"One of the greatest things
you can do in life is
walk around New York."

ROZ CHAST, *GOING INTO TOWN*

William J. Hennessey

Walking
Broadway

**Thirteen Miles of
Architecture and History**

THE MONACELLI PRESS

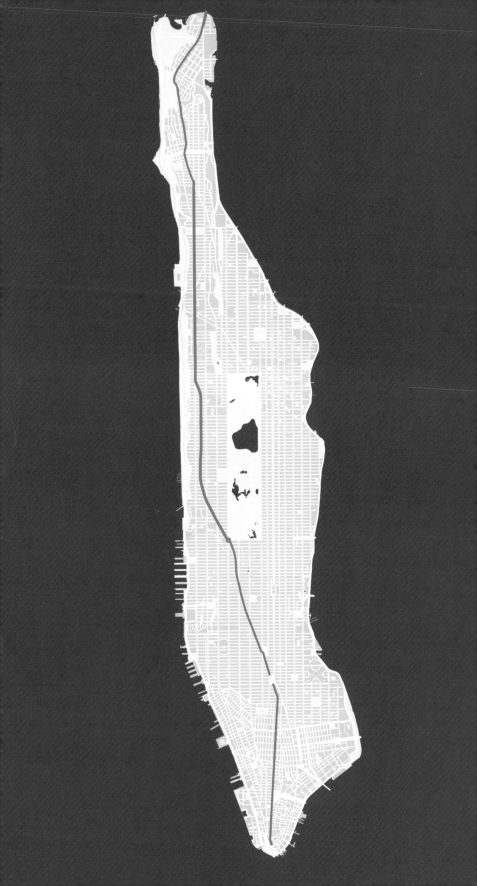

Contents

Preface

For most people, "Broadway" means show business—bright lights, glittering marquees, glamorous crowds, all the excitement that is part of the theater. This was certainly the case for me as a stage-struck teenager living in suburban New Jersey during the 1960s. Virtually every weekend I would hop on the train and head into the city to take my place among the standees at the back of a Broadway theater, haunt stage doors, or throw myself into acting classes in a creaky old studio in the tower above Carnegie Hall. I was in love with "Broadway" and determined to have a life in the theater.

As time passed, I discovered that there was more to New York than Broadway and more to Broadway than the theater district. I began to spend Saturday mornings before a matinee wandering the streets, exploring neighborhoods and attempting to capture their look and feel in photographs. Along the way, I became curious about the varied architectural styles I encountered.

A plan began to take shape: I would walk the island from one end to the other. Starting at the Battery, I would follow Broadway all the way to the Bronx, tackling this nearly fourteen-mile trek of discovery in manageable segments. In the following months, I found myself spending more time walking and less standing at the back of the theater. But then the inevitabilities of teenage life intervened, and my progress slowed. The "Broadway Project" ultimately petered out somewhere around Houston Street. I departed for college, grad school, and a museum career. Now half a century later, my wife and I have moved back to the city we have always loved. What better moment to pick up where I left off?

So, what kind of a book is this? On the most fundamental level it's about walking and looking, about observing and wondering. It's also a book about a specific street, focused on what we can see and experience in real time as we walk. Finally, this is a book for both fireside and curb side, designed both to be read at home and to be taken out as a guide to the streets.

In our daily lives, we set out on foot for a variety of reasons—to get to work, to run errands, for exercise, or for the pleasure of a relaxing stroll. No matter what its impetus, a walk can be a journey of discovery. When we walk, we can set our own pace. We may press briskly ahead toward a destination, or choose to amble, pausing whenever we like to look up or down or around. We give ourselves permission to study things in time, not just in passing. As we move along, structures catch our eye and prompt questions: "What an interesting/peculiar place. I wonder what it is." "Why is it here?" "What goes on inside?" "Who built it?" "When?" "Why does it look that way?" "Would I like it better if I knew more about it?" As we walk, our impressions of individual buildings coalesce into an overall sense of the personality of a neighborhood or district. We gain an understanding of how the city grew and developed and why neighborhoods, the villages that make up the metropolis, look and feel the way they do.

In the end, this is a book about the experience of looking at and thinking about the architecture of a remarkable city—building by building, block by block. And what better way to proceed than with a series of walks up New York's oldest and longest avenue?

View north on Broadway with the spire of
Trinity Church and the American Surety
Building, 1920.

Broadway:
A Historic Overview

Manhattan is famous for its grid—a uniform lattice of streets and avenues imposed more or less arbitrarily on the landscape. Broadway, the city's longest thoroughfare, does not conform. It snakes its way up the island in an irregular diagonal, following indigenous trails, natural topography, and economic opportunity rather than a map-maker's imperative.

Most of us think of Broadway as running the entire length of present-day Manhattan, all the way from the Battery to the Bronx. To be accurate, however, this great street does not start at what is now the southernmost tip of Manhattan (this is largely landfill), but a few blocks north at Bowling Green. Here in Manhattan's first public park is a perfect place for an historic overview of how Broadway's path evolved.

The story begins sometime around 1640 when the Dutch, in residence since 1624, built a road northward from their primitive fort and trading post near what was then the tip of Manhattan Island. The road was the Heere Straat, the main street of seventeenth-century Nieuw Amsterdam. In laying out the route, the Dutch followed a long-established trail used by the native Weckquaesgeek/Lenape peoples along a low ridge of land that moved northward. Unusually wide and straight, the Heere Straat quickly became the best address in Nieuw Amsterdam. The road terminated at a defensive stockade, now the foot of Wall Street.

When the English took over from the Dutch in 1664, Heere Straat was renamed the Broad Way. In those days, before landfill created what is now Tribeca and the area around the World Trade Center, the Broad Way ran up the west side of Manhattan island fairly close to the Hudson River. By the 1760s the Broad Way had been extended north to Thomas Street. By 1795 it had reached what is now Canal Street, and in 1801 the city's Common Council resolved that the street should be extended further north to what is now Union Square. There it would intersect with the city's other great north–south boulevard, Bowery Lane. For most of this stretch, Broadway's path is straight.

By 1820, when city surveyor John Randel published his meticulously detailed ninety-two-sheet map of Manhattan Island north of what is now Houston Street, the path that Broadway would eventually follow could clearly be discerned. On the Randel map, Broad Way comes to a stop at what is now Tenth Street. At this point the road angles off slightly to the west and takes on a new name: Bloomingdale Road. This meandering thoroughfare follows the high ground on the west side of Manhattan through what is now Midtown to the hamlets of Harsenville (now the west 70s), Stryker's Bay (86th to 96th Streets), Bloomingdale (centered around 110th Street), Manhattanville (120s), to Carmanville (140s). At what is now 143rd Street, the Bloomingdale Road veers to the east. Four blocks later it merges with another old highway, Kings Bridge Road. This highway descends into a valley at the center of the island to run all the way to an eponymous bridge over the Harlem River. This is essentially the route of what would become Broadway.

As the city grew northward and as the name Broadway was attached to successive sections of the Bloomingdale Road, the City Commissioners did their best to impose some order on the march of progress and development. Their efforts were only partly successful. Sections of the route were straightened, but the unruly diagonal that disrupted what John Randel called the "beautiful uniformity" of the Manhattan street grid was a fact of life. The intersection of that diagonal with the gridded north–south avenues produced what would become the series of squares—Union, Madison, Herald, Times— that define neighborhoods in the modern city.

By the 1860s, official maps of Manhattan show a continuous avenue running from Bowling Green all the way to Spuyten Duyvil Creek at the top of the island. The names applied to this thoroughfare, however, changed along the way. Until 1868 the stretch of the avenue labeled Broadway stopped at what would become Columbus Circle. In that year the city adopted a plan to create "the Boulevard," a wide Parisian-style avenue with a central median extending north from 59th to 155th Street. The Boulevard's northern terminus marked the spot where the 1811 Commissioner's Plan for New York City's grid stopped. For the most part, the Boulevard ran in a straight line following the basic route of the old Bloomingdale Road. As commercial development continued northward, the Boulevard was extended to 169th Street, where it merged with the Kings Bridge Road. Finally, in 1899, the entire route stretching from Bowling Green to the Harlem River was officially renamed Broadway.

Using This Book

This book is organized geographically as a series of fourteen walks, starting in the south at Bowling Green and moving north. The walks are of different lengths and correspond to distinct stretches of Broadway. Each is a manageable stroll in itself, and walks can be combined or broken into smaller segments, depending on the day and your mood. Many can be supplemented by shorter walks or detours to interested buildings "off Broadway" to the east or west. These walks are detailed on the blue pages. Subway connections along the route are noted on the maps.

Identifying Buildings

Individual buildings can be known by multiple names: address (25 Broadway), builder or principal tenant (Woolworth Building), various owners over time (International Mercantile Marine Building), or their marketing nickname (1 Liberty Plaza). Both the current street address and the name of the original or most notable owner of the building are given.

Later or alternative names are given in parentheses. You will quickly notice that odd numbered buildings along Broadway are on the west side of the street. Even numbers are on the east. For buildings that are individual New York City landmarks, the name used in the official city designation is given. Many of these buildings bear bronze plaques installed by the New York Community Trust or the New York Landmarks Preservation Foundation that provide useful historical information. As you walk, watch the color of the street signs. When they turn from green to brown, you have entered a designated historic district.

Scaffolding

At this writing the city's department of buildings lists over 3500 sidewalk sheds along Manhattan streets. On many buildings scaffolding covers the entire facade. Some of this scaffolding enables renovation and adaptive reuse of older buildings. Some is necessary for regular cleaning and repair, much of which is legally mandated. On May 16, 1979, a section of the cornice on a building on West 115th Street fell to the street, tragically killing a Barnard College student. In response, the City enacted Local Laws 10 and 11, requiring facade inspections every five years for all structures taller than six stories.

This means that a large number of interesting buildings are under wraps at any given time, making their architectural detailing virtually invisible. This is frustrating, but it's a fact of life. For some buildings we simply have to come back later.

Access to Interiors

Along the route, many interesting spaces, such as churches, office building lobbies, event venues, and government buildings are not regularly open to the public. Sometimes all it takes is a polite request to gain access, sometimes signing up for a formal tour is the best or only option, and sometimes it's just a question of timing. The annual Open House New York weekend is also a wonderful opportunity to see places that are not normally accessible.

Look Up

The lower floors of New York buildings are frequently modified to accommodate new retail tenants and seldom look today the way they did when the building first opened. The best part of a building is very often at the top. Architects frequently lavished their most creative efforts there. Look up. And don't forget to cross the street. It's often easier to take in a building from a distance than from up close.

Buildings also often look very different in morning and afternoon light. As the sun moves from one side of the street to the other, raking light allows previously obscure architectural details to stand out in dramatic relief. Finally, as you plan your outings, remember that Broadway is a busy street, nearly always packed with traffic and pedestrians. Weekends may offer some relief, but be prepared to have lots of company.

OCTOBER 19, 1978 ★ NEW YORK YANKEES, WORLD SERIES CHAMPIONS

Look Down

Along the initial sections of Broadway, from Bowling Green north to City Hall, you will notice a series of bronze lettered strips embedded in the sidewalk. Each of these honors an individual, a group, or an event commemorated by a ticker tape parade, a great New York tradition. More than 200 such celebratory parades have been held since 1886. Today the stock ticker has gone the way of the typewriter and adding machine. The city is obliged to provide and distribute confetti to ensure an appropriate storm of flying paper for contemporary parades.

Take Pictures

Consider bringing along a camera. Not only does this provide an easy way to document the journey and remember favorite buildings, but photography can be a great aid to seeing. The act of thoughtfully composing a satisfying photograph, one that captures the essence of a building, is an effective way to develop an understanding of that structure and the way it works within its urban context.

Fulton

Vesey

Church

17 🚇 **19**

🚇 Dey

18

John

Cortlandt

Maiden Lane

16

Liberty

Nassau

Cedar

15

Thames

14

12

Pine

13

11

Trinity Place

Wall

10

🚇 Rector

9

8

Exchange Place

7

New

6

5

Beaver

4

3

Bowling Green

2

Stone

1

Bridge

Pearl

Water

State

Whitehall

Broadway

1. Alexander Hamilton Custom House
2. International Mercantile Marine Building
3. Bowling Green Offices
4. Cunard Building
5. Standard Oil Building
6. 29 Broadway
7. 45 Broadway Atrium and 55 Broadway
8. The American Express Building
9. The Empire Building
10. 1 Wall Street (Irving Trust Building)
11. Trinity Church
12. Trinity Building
13. American Surety Building
14. Equitable Building
15. Marine Midland Bank Building
16. 165 Broadway (1 Liberty Plaza)
17. American Telephone and Telegraph Building
18. Corbin Building
19. Fulton Center

WALK 1

Bowling Green to Fulton Street

Our walk begins at the foot of Broadway in Bowling Green. This is New York's oldest park, established in 1733 "for the Beauty & Ornament of the Said Street (i.e., Broadway) as well as for the Recreation & delight of the Inhabitants of this City." It's still a lovely oasis and it is a good spot from which to consider the first buildings on our tour, beginning with the monumental United States Custom House.

❶ Alexander Hamilton Custom House

Bowling Green

1899–1907 · CASS GILBERT

Before the imposition of a national income tax, tariffs and cargo duties were the largest source of revenue for the federal government. It was in this building that most of these fees were tallied and collected.

The Custom House was built on the site of Fort Amsterdam, erected by the Dutch to protect one of the world's great natural harbors. By 1790 the fort had been replaced by Government House, intended to be the home of the President when New York was the nation's capital. (The year after it was completed, the capital relocated to Philadelphia. George Washington never had the chance to move in.) By the late nineteenth century, the area was a hub of maritime commerce, the logical site for a custom house large enough to accommodate the growing needs of America's busiest port.

At the center of the facade, paired engaged Corinthian columns flank a triumphal portal crowned with a cartouche by Karl Bitter. To the left and right, large plinths support the *Four Continents* by Daniel Chester French. Each group is replete with traditional symbols and attributes. To the east is the haughty figure of *Asia*, seated on a throne of skulls and flanked by exhausted captives. Next comes *America*, alert, energetic, and focused on the future. She is accompanied by eagles and a subservient Native American. *Europe*, looking regal and confident, holds a globe signifying her conquests and dominion. Her throne is decorated with scenes from the frieze of the Parthenon. In contrast, *Africa* to the west slumbers between a sphinx and a lion. Twelve figures representing great seafaring centers (including Greece, Phoenicia, Genoa, Venice, Holland) at the attic level and a series of allegorical carved heads on the keystones of the main floor windows complete the sculptural program.

Imposing steps lead up to an arched entry decorated with bands of mosaics in blue and gold. Bronze doors open onto a richly embellished entrance hall. Nautical motifs are everywhere. Today the building houses a branch of the Smithsonian's Museum of the American Indian, New York's Bankruptcy Court, and the local office of the National Archives.

On the main floor, facing Bowling Green, is the Collector's Office. The most lushly decorated suite in the building, it features elaborate woodwork, an imposing fireplace, painted port scenes by Elmer Garnsey, and decoration by Tiffany Studios—all arrayed under a deeply coffered gold ceiling. This is a splendid room, appropriate to the powerful (and lucrative) office of Collector.

The focus of the interior is a central rotunda, directly on axis with the main entry. This huge elliptical room is astonishing in its drama and confidence. Overhead, a large oval skylight set into a shallow dome (designed by the Spanish engineer Rafael Guastavino) illuminates the former customs clerks' work area behind the counter.

Around the dome are paintings added in 1937 by Reginald Marsh, working under the sponsorship of the WPA Treasury Relief Art Project. Marsh and his assistants took full advantage of the dome's curving profile to create compositions that capture the romance of maritime life in Depression-era New York. Ocean liners pass the Ambrose Lightship and are wrestled into their berths by tugs. Stevedores unload cargo, and celebrity passengers are interviewed by eager reporters.

The corner of Broadway and Battery Place marks the start of "Steamship Row." By the mid-1920s New York controlled fully 80 percent of the transatlantic passenger traffic. This first stretch of Broadway was home to the multiple shipping companies competing for that business.

❷ International Mercantile Marine Building
(later United States Lines Building)

1 Broadway

1919–21 · WALTER BOUGHTON CHAMBERS

In 1902 J. P. Morgan assembled a group of six English and American shipping lines into a single maritime holding company, the largest merchant fleet in the world. The company included the White Star Line, owners of the *Titanic*. In 1919 the company purchased what was then called the Washington Building, built in 1882 by transatlantic cable pioneer Cyrus Field to the designs of Edward Kendall to serve as its headquarters. Architect Walter Boughton Chambers was recruited to update the structure.

Chambers reclad Kendall's red-brick building in Indiana limestone and removed most of the detail to create a lean, stripped down,

classical design that recalls the work of English architect Edwin Lutyens. To soften the building's severity and to incorporate some corporate advertising, Chambers added a row of shields on the second level highlighting the company's ports of call, including Plymouth, London, Queenstown, Melbourne, New York, and Capetown.

The main portal is enriched with figures of Neptune, Mercury, and assorted maritime motifs. The passenger booking hall entries, around the corner on Battery Place, are still marked First Class and Cabin Class. Third Class passengers were relegated to a basement entry on Greenwich Street.

❸ Bowling Green Offices

5–11 Broadway

1895–98 · WILLIAM JAMES AUDSLEY AND GEORGE ASHDOWN AUDSLEY

This was the home of International Mercantile Marine before the renovation of 1 Broadway. It was here that anxious relatives gathered in 1912 to learn the fate of passengers on the *Titanic*. The building also housed the American Line, the American Scanic Line, and a variety of ship builders, freight forwarders, and naval architects. Bowling Green Offices was one of the largest buildings in the city when it was completed; it is also a structure with a distinct and very appealing personality.

The designers, British in origin, were the authors of more than twenty-five books on traditional craftsmanship and ornament. Their expertise shows in the beautifully delineated and meticulously executed terra-cotta detailing here. The Audsleys described their style as Hellenic

Renaissance, "a free but pure treatment of ancient Greek architecture in which the spirit rather than the letter of that refined style is carried out." In a context of buildings with Roman pretentions or exuberant Beaux-Arts detailing, Bowling Green Offices does seem both "Grecian" and curiously modern in its decorative restraint and simple massing.

❹ Cunard Building

25 Broadway

1917–21· BENJAMIN WISTAR MORRIS WITH CARRÈRE & HASTINGS

The Cunard Building, the first major structure erected in New York after World War I, features two projecting wings flanking a recessed center pavilion rising from a rusticated ground floor. The facade is embellished with a Tuscan colonnade on the second story and rises to a handsome terminating loggia. Although the exterior of the building is austere, maritime sculptural accents by the partnership of Eugene Rochette & Michael Parzini liven things up. There are seahorses and riders crowning the two side pavilions at the setback level, roundels on the lower facade, and nautical keystones (Neptune and the Four Winds) over each of the entry arches.

At the center of the ground floor, three large rusticated arches and a handsome set of bronze doors open into the five-bay lobby. Overhead are richly detailed groin vaults with playful sculptural reliefs by Paul Jennewein—echoes of the Renaissance masters Verrocchio and Donatello.

From here, across a small passageway, the great expanse of the booking hall opens before us. This space, intended to rival the interiors of New York's great railway stations, was inspired equally by ancient Roman baths and by the richly decorated loggias of Renaissance villas. Extending the full depth of the building, the hall unfolds in three sections: two richly chromatic vaulted areas extended by niches, and an octagonal central area capped by a shallow dome rising sixty-five feet above the floor. Originally, sunshine flooded in through large thermal windows opening onto light courts at each side.

The decorative program appropriately features maritime motifs. In the spandrels under the arches are evocations of historic voyages of discovery by Columbus, Ericson, Cabot, and Drake painted by Ezra Winter. In the flanking spaces are large painted maps by Barry Faulkner showing Cunard's shipping routes. There are sculptural panels of sea monsters and tritons. A bronze compass by John Gregory is incorporated in the colorful mosaic floor. The iron gates and screens are the work of the great metalsmith Samuel Yellin. The effect is one of overwhelming opulence. Passengers who bought tickets here knew that their ocean passage was going to be something special.

Across the street, the dramatic curving facade of 26 Broadway provides a powerful visual counterpoint to Cunard's solid rectangular mass. Together these two buildings frame the canyon that Broadway becomes as it narrows and heads north. This is the start of the financial district.

❺ Standard Oil Building

26 Broadway
1884–85 · EBENEZER L. ROBERTS
1920–28 · THOMAS HASTINGS
WITH SHREVE, LAMB & BLAKE

John D. Rockefeller bought this site in 1884. The present structure is the product of a collaboration between Thomas Hastings and the firm of Shreve, Lamb & Blake (later, as Shreve, Lamb & Harmon, the firm designed the Empire State Building). The Standard Oil Building was erected in stages as land for expansion became available.

   This building is most interesting for its ingenious massing. The architects were among the first to attempt a large office building in Lower Manhattan after the adoption of the 1916 building code, which mandated that the upper stories of tall buildings be set back to ensure that light and air reached the ground below. In addition, the architects were faced with the challenge of accommodating Broadway's strong curve as the street heads north. Their solution was to give the Standard Oil Building a dynamic twist part way up. At street level the large curving base with its two wings separated by a deep south-facing light court sweeps along Broadway. Up above, a square setback tower, modeled on the ancient Hellenistic Mausoleum of Halicarnassus, rises from the curving base. In a bold stroke, the architects rotated the tower's axis to align with the Manhattan street grid.

At ground level, the building is a powerful contributor to the canyon-like drama of lower Broadway. From a distance, the tower, nearly invisible from the street, becomes an integral part of the Manhattan skyline. The complex interplay of these two components can best be seen from Battery Park or Bowling Green.

❻ 29 Broadway

1929–31 · SLOAN & ROBERTSON

Compared with its neighbors, 29 Broadway is a mere sliver, but it's a sliver with style. The Broadway facade is little more than the entry to a much larger building back on Trinity Place. The architects exploited the narrow site that gave them the coveted Broadway address. Over the entry portal, a stacked column of single windows leads the eye upward. To the left, the remaining windows are extended horizontally by dark brick bands that draw our gaze around the corner and down Morris Street toward the main block of the building. The lobby may be the best thing about the structure. Take a look inside at the elegant use of polished metal, aluminum leaf, and pale marble to create an art deco symphony in shades of gray, white, and silver.

❼ 45 Broadway Atrium and 55 Broadway

1982–84 · FOX & FOWLE

Here are two wonderfully complementary buildings, siblings separated at birth by a fast-food restaurant. While the developers here would have much preferred to erect a single building, their failure to acquire a crucial piece of property forced them to turn an awkward situation to their advantage. The architects created two elevations as a study in counterpoint. The sharp angles and crisp corners of one structure set against the soft flowing curves of the other provide far more visual interest than would have been generated by a single building. And in an area

dominated by limestone and marble, it's a relief to see such handsome use of brick. The blank south facade of 55 Broadway is enlivened with spirited patterning, improving the view for the neighbors.

❽ American Express Building

65 Broadway

1914–17 · JAMES L. ASPINWALL OF RENWICK, ASPINWALL & TUCKER

The American Express Building is a good reminder that along this stretch of Broadway it's often as rewarding to look up as it is

to scan from side to side. Nearly every building displays some sort of classical arch, temple, or portico at its crest. Here, high above the dignified Corinthian columns and arcaded entry, is a bridge connecting the two wings of the building. It is as if a giant took hold of a Roman triumphal arch and stretched it skyward. An eagle cartouche at the top echoes the agitated bronze bird that has alighted over the main entrance. This was the corporation's original logo, before it adopted the current gladiator.

❾ Empire Building

71 Broadway

1895–98 · FRANCIS KIMBALL OF KIMBALL & THOMPSON

The architect of the Empire Building was lucky to have two facades on which to display his skill. The long Rector Street elevation, overlooking Trinity Churchyard, is a balanced, Renaissance-inspired, composition that terminates in a richly plastic loggia and a generous sheltering cornice. On either side of the main entrance, steps leading down to the subway and lower level shops provide an urban grace note. The calm poise of the four eagles flanking the Broadway entrance is a pleasant alternative to the irritable American Express bird next door.

Broadway and Wall Street, two of New York's most celebrated streets, intersect up ahead. The spot is a distinguished one both because of its architecture and its history. For years the corner was considered New York's most valuable piece of real estate. Trinity Church, New York's oldest parish, has occupied its site on the west side of Broadway since 1698. Down Wall Street to the east is the spot where George Washington was inaugurated as our first president in 1789. Three years later what was to become the New York Stock exchange was founded under a buttonwood tree nearby.

⑩ 1 Wall Street
(Irving Trust Building)

1928–32 · RALPH T. WALKER OF
VOORHEES, GMELIN & WALKER

This is a very fine building at
a very glamorous address.
Architect Ralph Walker produced
an assured and elegant
structure. Smooth and taut, it
shoots up a full fifty stories
through a series of carefully
calculated setbacks. From some
angles, the building resembles
a highly abstracted fluted column; from others it looks like a giant
mineral crystal.

Every detail contributes to the overall effect. The facade is subtly
sculpted with precise chamfered, knife-edge corners. Deliberate
variations in the spacing of the vertical piers and the undulations of the
surface suggest an almost musical rhythm. Windows are set deeply
into the facade and shaped to conform to the curve of the stone skin
so as not to interfere with the upward vertical flow or with the geometric
precision of the massing. Where ornament is used, it is shallow and
clings closely to the surface.

This one-time bank headquarters is being converted into
condominiums, and its theatrical main entrance facing onto the narrow
canyon of Wall Street and its glorious gilded lobby are buried under
scaffolding. The art deco tower above continues to engage in a lively
conversation with the venerable spire of Trinity Church across Broadway.

⑪ Trinity Church

75 Broadway

1839–46 · RICHARD UPJOHN

For many years after it was completed in 1846, the spire of Trinity
Church was the tallest structure in Manhattan. That, of course,
has changed. But the church still occupies a special place among
New York's monuments. It would be hard to imagine a building
more intimately connected with the growth of the city. The present
church is the third on this site.

Trinity's churchyard is a leafy refuge amid the noise and crowds of lower Broadway. Extraordinary people are buried here: Robert Fulton, Albert Gallatin, and Alexander Hamilton, to name a few.

Unlike its neighbors, Trinity was constructed of a velvety sandstone, slightly lighter in color than the brownstone used for mid-nineteenth century row houses. The material is particularly well-handled at Trinity. The shifting shades of the various stone blocks add life and variety to the walls. The warm stone is a pleasant counterpoint to the cool formality of this marble and limestone neighborhood.

Upjohn's tower for Trinity Church warrants special attention. From a powerfully solid base pierced by the main portal, it rises upward through a large lancet window to a gilded clock and bell loft before making an effortless transition to the octagonal spire. The spirited statues of the four evangelists on the north and south faces are the work of the English sculptors William Farmer and William Brindley.

Now enter the church through the bronze doors designed by Richard Morris Hunt and executed by Karl Bitter. Inside, the broad nave unfolds with a gracious, relaxed rhythm moving our gaze toward the large stained-glass window. Overhead, the complex lierne vaulting provides a lively counterpoint to the calmer rhythm of the walls with their carefully balanced areas of unadorned plaster and decorative trim. By design, the interior is largely free from tombs, memorials, and other sculptural interventions. The one exception is the richly Victorian altar and reredos designed by Frederick Clarke Withers in 1876 as a memorial to real estate magnate William Backhouse Astor.

⑫ Trinity Building

111 Broadway
1904–7 · FRANCIS KIMBALL OF
KIMBALL & THOMPSON

Francis Kimball's office building
overlooking Trinity Churchyard
pays appropriate stylistic homage
to its famous neighbor. Inspired
by Upjohn's use of the Gothic
Revival, Kimball created what is
probably the first Gothic-inspired
skyscraper, starting a vogue that
found its greatest expression a
few blocks north in the Woolworth Building. For Kimball, Gothic was a
loose term. The architect invented his own version of the Middle
Ages, just as he did with the Renaissance in the Empire Building on
the south side of Trinity Church. In the Trinity Building round and
pointed arches coexist happily with medieval and Renaissance-inspired
ornament to surprisingly harmonious effect.

Both the Trinity Building and its fraternal twin, the **U.S. Realty
Building** at 115 Broadway, also designed by Kimball and completed the
same year as Trinity, are slender twenty-one story slabs, erected on
very narrow sites. Their height turns Thames Street between them into
a canyon of notable gloom. High above the street there is a tiny elegant
bridge linking the two buildings.

The turret of the Trinity Building, on the angled facade at the corner
of Broadway and Thames Street, adds a dynamic asymmetry to the
design. Note the sumptuous gilt-bronze tracery on the entry doors and
the handsome vaulting overhead.

⑬ The American Surety Building

100 Broadway
1894–96 · BRUCE PRICE

The American Surety Building was among the first to embrace the
classical column with its three component parts (base, shaft, capital)
as a useful analog for skyscraper design. The idea was championed
by the influential architectural critic Montgomery Schuyler, and once
it took hold, the formula was to remain the standard for nearly twenty

years. When it was built, 100 Broadway was freestanding, a proud tower unengaged by other buildings.

Price's original design was beautifully proportioned and fully detailed on all four sides. The building was widened in 1921 and renovated in the 1970s. Along the way, the original proportions were altered, and it became hemmed in by other structures. But we still can enjoy the expressive volutes on the Ionic capitals and J. Massey Rhind's row of classical maidens standing with stolid dignity above the columns framing the entry. The doorway at the south end of the facade (part of the 1921 addition) is also worth a look, as is the beautiful crown.

⓮ Equitable Building

120 Broadway

1913–15 · ERNEST R. GRAHAM & ASSOCIATES (SUCCESSORS TO D. H. BURNHAM & COMPANY)

This stretch of Broadway was long identified with the insurance industry, which enjoyed explosive growth in the early years of the twentieth century. Perhaps no company grew so quickly as Equitable. At the time of its completion, its headquarters at 120 Broadway was the largest office building in the world: thirty-eight stories tall, arranged in a tight H plan, and rising skyward without a break.

Like the American Surety Building, the Equitable Building's design is based on the tripartite column form. Its classical base at street level gives way to a multi-story shaft and then to a differentiated crowning element at the top. But this is neither a skyline building nor one that seeks to enhance corporate prestige through fine materials, sculptural embellishment, or decorative detailing. The

Equitable Building was a speculative venture, designed to incorporate as much rentable square footage onto a building lot as possible. Its extraordinary bulk was the catalyst for the creation of the city's first building code. Enacted in 1916 to regulate the height and design of office buildings, the code set limits on a building's massing, mandated setbacks, and limited total square footage to a sensible multiple of lot size. With the 1916 code in place, the model for tall buildings in New York changed, and the setback tower replaced the column form as the standard for skyscraper design.

⓰ Marine Midland Bank Building

140 Broadway

1964–67 · GORDON BUNSHAFT OF SKIDMORE, OWINGS & MERRILL

In 1961 New York substantially updated its zoning rules. The new Zoning Resolution reflected the influence of continuing suburbanization, renewed concerns about the impact of urban density, and major shifts in the basis of the city's economy.

The key feature of the 1961 Resolution was the introduction of incentive zoning. Developers who agreed to set their buildings back from the street to create public plazas (POPS – Privately Owned Public Space) were allowed to add extra floors. An easing of setback requirements allowed builders to erect sleek steel and glass towers that rose unbroken from the pavement. Inside, vast expanses of open floor area allowed a new flexibility in office layout not available in setback towers.

As a result, the prevailing aesthetic of tight urban canyons with tall buildings hugging their lot lines gave way to a less rigid sequence of "towers in a park." 140 Broadway is a near-perfect example of the new paradigm—an unadorned slab set well back from the street rising fifty-two stories straight up from a paved plaza. The building is sheathed tightly in a thin, suave skin of tinted glass. Through the dark glass are tantalizing glimpses of the interior, of people at work, and of the carefully considered ceiling light fixtures,

very much a part of the design. With subtlety and refinement, the architect has carefully balanced transparency and reflection.

Isamu Noguchi's *Red Cube*, positioned with great precision on the plaza, is a crucial part of the composition, adding a vivid crimson counterpoint to the sober bronze and black of the building. Just as 140 Broadway itself is not a rectangle, but a more dynamic trapezoid in shape, Noguchi's slightly distorted *Red Cube* is balanced on end so that it appears simultaneously precarious and weightless.

⑯ 165 Broadway
1 Liberty Plaza

1971–74 · SKIDMORE, OWINGS & MERRILL

Looking at the structural material of this hulking giant, it is no surprise that it was built as a commercial project by U.S. Steel. The building is a potent advertisement for the product: a pile of massive plate girders pierced by small slit-like windows and surrounded by a moat-like sunken plaza. Regrettably, the construction of 165 Broadway required the demolition of one of New York's greatest early skyscrapers: Ernest Flagg's elegant Singer Building of 1907.

On the southwest corner of Broadway and Liberty Street is **Zuccotti Park**. The open space was originally created in 1968 as POPS—part of the zoning deal that allowed US Steel to add bonus stories to its building across the street. Seriously damaged in the World Trade Center attack, the park was restored and reopened in 2006. At that time it was renamed for John Zuccotti, former City Planning Commissioner and chairman of Brookfield Properties, which is responsible for so much of the retail redevelopment around the World Trade Center site. Zuccotti Park was the hub of the Occupy Wall Street Movement in 2011. At the corner the brilliant crimson sculpture *Joie de Vivre* by Mark di Suvero addresses Noguchi's *Red Cube.*

⑰ American Telephone and Telegraph Building

195 Broadway

1912–22 · WILLIAM WELLES BOSWORTH

17

195 Broadway is neither a tripartite, column-inspired building nor a set-back tower. An extraordinarily dignified Doric arcade at ground level is surmounted by a three-story Ionic colonnade, then another, and another, and another—eight in total. At the northwest corner atop an architecturally distinct tower is a small replica of the Halicarnassus mausoleum. A colossal gilded statue of the *Genius of Electricity* once stood atop the mausoleum.

Bosworth and AT&T worked hard to erect a building that evoked corporate dignity and permanence. Something of a scholar, Bosworth drew nearly all his details from specific ancient Greek architectural sources. He sought out first-rate building materials, insisted on quality construction, and engaged noted artists as partners. Replicas of Paul Manship's bronze panels of the four elements are installed over the entries on the Broadway facade. The originals are now in the Philadelphia Museum of Art.

The current entrance to the main lobby is around the corner on Dey Street. Here Bosworth has created a forest of solid Doric columns, a true Greek hypostyle hall. There is a fine coffered ceiling, and along the frieze there are sculptural reliefs by Manship and Gaston Lachaise.

⑱ Corbin Building

192 Broadway

1888–89 · FRANCIS KIMBALL OF KIMBALL & THOMPSON

18

The Corbin Building takes full advantage of its narrow corner site. The architect has combined a jaunty smorgasbord of past architectural styles (Gothic,

Renaissance, François Premier, English Victorian) and a rich variety of building materials (brick, Long Meadow sandstone, terra-cotta, cast iron) into a dramatic and pleasing whole that is warm in color and texture. From its narrow twenty-foot frontage on Broadway, the building shoots along the full length of John Street. Continuous horizontal cornices accentuate the perspective effect and make the building seem even longer than it is.

⑲ Fulton Center

200 Broadway

2005–14 · NICHOLAS GRIMSHAW AND JAMES CARPENTER DESIGN ASSOCIATES

Next door to the Corbin Building and attached to it is this major transportation hub providing access to eleven subway lines. The Fulton Center shows that it is possible to surmount huge engineering and logistical challenges to create a facility that handles vast numbers of passengers while providing them with some glamour and visual excitement along the way. It's worth going down the stairs for the chance to stand under the station's dramatic oculus. *Sky Reflector Net* uses hundreds of small metal mirrors to direct sunlight down four stories into the subway station below.

Look west along Fulton Street. You will be treated to a dramatic view of the One World Trade Center Freedom Tower. The wings of Santiago Calatrava's Oculus transportation hub jut out over the street from the south.

Howard

Canal

Lispenard

Walker

White

Franklin

Leonard

Worth

Thomas

Duane

Reade

Chambers

Warren

Murray

Barclay

Vesey

Fulton

Dey

Cortlandt

Maiden Lane

Church

Broadway

Lafayette

Centre

Park Row

Ann

Nassau

Centre

Church

❶ St. Paul's Chapel

❷ Park Row Building

❸ Woolworth Building

❹ Home Life Insurance Building

❺ Rogers, Peet Building

❻ City Hall Park

❼ City Hall Station

❽ City Hall

Ⓐ "Tweed" Courthouse

Ⓑ Municipal Building

Ⓒ Surrogates Court/Hall of Records

❾ Broadway Chambers Building

❿ A. T. Stewart Store

⓫ 287 Broadway

⓬ East River Savings Institution

⓭ Barclay Building

⓮ Ted Weiss Federal Building

⓯ Javits Office Building

⓰ Mutual Reserve Building

⓱ Fire Engine Company 7 and Hook and Ladder Company 1

⓲ 319 Broadway

⓳ 8 Thomas Street

⓴ 325 Broadway

㉑ New York Life Insurance Building

㉒ Thompson's Saloon

㉓ James White Building

㉔ 366 Broadway

㉕ 380 Broadway

㉖ Grosvenor Building

㉗ 388 Broadway

㉘ 400 Broadway

㉙ 415 Broadway

Fulton Street to Canal Street

The personality of the next section of Broadway evolves as it moves north. We begin at St. Paul's Chapel, an important landmark of old New York, move on to City Hall and the buildings of municipal government, and then enter what was in the nineteenth century the center of mercantile activity in the city and the site of some of its early skyscrapers.

Until the twentieth century, Broadway was the home of New York's tallest buildings. From the time of its completion in 1846 until 1890, Trinity Church was the loftiest structure in the city. Trinity lost this distinction when Joseph Pulitzer erected his New York World Building on City Hall Park. The Manhattan Life Building at 64 Broadway eclipsed the World Building in 1894, only to be overshadowed in 1899 by the Park Row Building.

The Flatiron Building at 23rd Street claimed the crown in 1902, to be overtaken in turn by Ernest Flagg's Singer Building at Liberty Street six years later. The Metropolitan Life Building opened in 1909 and was then surpassed by the Woolworth Building in 1915. It enjoyed its supremacy until 1930. Each of these buildings either stood on or overlooked Broadway. Five of them survive today, and we will look at them all.

❶ St. Paul's Chapel

209 Broadway
1764–66 · STEEPLE 1794–96, JAMES CROMMELIN LAWRENCE

St. Paul's is Manhattan's oldest public building in continuous use. Built as a "Chapel of Ease" for Trinity Church, St. Paul's offered convenience to those who felt that they were just not up to the six-block walk south to the main church. The building sits today surrounded by a handsome iron fence in a well-kept churchyard. Saint Paul's has always

been a busy place. After the great fire of 1776 that destroyed Trinity's main building, St. Paul's became New York's premier place of worship. It was here that George Washington went to pray following his inauguration in 1789. More than two hundred years later, after the September 11 attacks in 2001, St. Paul's, miraculously undamaged, became a support and rest center for rescue workers. Inside at the west end of the church, the 9/11 Chapel of Remembrance recalls St. Paul's remarkable role in the city's recovery.

The design of St. Paul's was directly inspired by that of James Gibbs's London church of St. Martin in the Fields (1722–24). St. Paul's, however, is built of humbler materials—roughly cut Manhattan schist with brownstone quoins and window dressings. This gives the building an appealingly sturdy, almost rustic charm. Even though it was readily available, the local schist stone which underlies so much of Manhattan was rarely used as a building material. It just seemed too rough and ready.

Originally St. Paul's looked to the Hudson River. Parishioners entered from the churchyard under the tower and proceeded eastward towards the altar. As Broadway increased in importance during the 1770s, the decision was made to shift the main entry to the portico at the east end so that the public face of the church opened to Broadway.

Inside, thanks to a recent restoration that returned the interior to the original white and beige color scheme, St. Paul's is pleasingly light and open, a lovely and very eighteenth-century space. Tall Corinthian columns with stilted entablature blocks support an elliptically vaulted nave. There are dark wood galleries, tall arched windows in the aisles, and at the east end a very handsome Palladian window. After the Revolutionary War, a monument to American General Richard

Montgomery was installed outside under the portico directly in front of this window. French architect Pierre Charles l'Enfant, famous for his plan of Washington, D.C., was hired to design an altarpiece to mask the shadow cast by the monument. The original box pews have been removed to create an open and flexible space that is used for worship and as the setting for performances by the highly regarded Trinity Wall Street Choir and Trinity Baroque Orchestra.

At Vesey Street, Broadway widens to meet City Hall Park. Park Row angles off to the east. That street was once the home to nearly every one of New York's major newspapers: the *World, Tribune, Times,* and *Herald* were all here. All have now relocated or closed up shop. The impressive Park Row Building remains on the corner of Park Row and Ann Street.

❷ Park Row Building

15 Park Row

1899 · R. H. ROBERTSON

From 1899 to 1908, the Park Row Building was the tallest in the city, but the imposing structure seems ambivalent about its height. Instead of soaring boldly skyward, the building's vertical momentum is diminished by Robertson's decision to group floors into horizontal units separated by cornices and balconies. Be sure to stand back far enough to get a good look at the two copper-clad cupolas and the richly detailed ornamental balconies as well as the four figures by J. Massey Rhind looking out to Broadway. The Park Row Building has a very irregular plan. It's worth walking around back to compare the stark austerity and unrelenting plainness of the side elevations to the richly articulated main facade.

❸ Woolworth Building

In 1879 Frank Woolworth opened his first 5 & 10-cent store in Utica, New York. The concept was a novel one—nothing cost more than a dime, and customers were expected to select their own merchandise from bins, rather than having it presented to them by a clerk. The idea was a success, and by 1918 there would be over 1,000 Woolworth stores on both sides of the Atlantic.

After moving from upstate New York to Manhattan in 1886, Woolworth established his offices in rented space just north of City Hall. He soon began to plan for a building of his own. Woolworth envisioned a structure that would be a distinctive landmark, a powerful advertisement for the company, the tallest building in the world.

Two thirty-story wings fill the entire block front along Broadway from Barclay Street to Park Place. From the center of this mass, the tower rises an additional thirty stories, culminating in a glorious pyramidal roof and lantern flanked by four tourelles. The ensemble is beautifully proportioned, and Gilbert achieved a dynamic balance between the inherent power of the overall mass and the delicacy of the historical detailing.

On an early business trip to London, Woolworth had been deeply impressed by Charles Barry and A. W. N. Pugin's New Palace of Westminster. He asked Gilbert if this secular version of the Gothic style might be used for their tower. Gilbert agreed, and although the Woolworth Building was early dubbed a "Cathedral of Commerce," the architect was explicit that neither he nor Woolworth sought to evoke ecclesiastical associations.

The first four stories of the building are clad in limestone; everything above is terra-cotta. The material was chosen because it is light, fireproof, comparatively inexpensive, easy to cast in detail, and because

it takes color beautifully. Gilbert skillfully exploited the latter property, using tints of cream, rose, and blue to dramatize the building's ascent and to accentuate the effect of naturally occurring shadows on the surface.

Gilbert envisioned the lobby as a grand public space. Four golden Roman barrel-vaulted arcades converge at a central crossing. Elevator banks are placed to the north and south, and there were originally shops lining the lobby walls. Straight ahead and opposite the main entry a monumental marble staircase once drew visitors to a bank lobby on the mezzanine level.

The overall effect of the lobby is sumptuous. Reflective materials are used throughout: dark polished wood, bronze, colored marble, stained glass. There are mural representations of Commerce and Labor on the north and south balconies. Sly portraits of Woolworth himself (holding nickels and dimes), Gilbert (with a model of the building), the bank president, the structural engineer, and other luminaries decorate the carved corbels.

Woolworth's building cost $13.5 million. The owner paid in cash. He got his money's worth. The building is the perfect embodiment of the early twentieth-century skyscraper. It is rational in its planning and engineering, romantic in its height and ambition, sophisticated and refined in its decoration.

❹ Home Life Insurance Building

256–57 Broadway

1892–94 · PIERRE LE BRUN OF NAPOLEON LE BRUN & SONS

This is a classic base-shaft-capital building executed in a style loosely derived from Renaissance Flanders. The rusticated ground floor yields to a richly decorated and arched piano nobile. This level in turn gives way to a balanced shaft interrupted at intervals by balconies. The composition culminates in a deep, two-tiered loggia, even more richly decorated with reliefs, that supports an arcade below a steep pyramidal roof. The entire facade is constructed of Tuckahoe marble.

Next door is the dignified **Rogers, Peet Building ❺** at 258 Broadway. Completed in 1900 by architect John B. Snook for the celebrated men's clothier, the facade clearly expresses the underlying steel structure.

Directly across Broadway is **City Hall Park ❻**. In colonial Dutch and English days, the park was common land offering both shared pasture and an open space for civic events. In 1803, when work began on City Hall, it became a public park. Thoughtfully restored in 1999, City Hall Park today is a lovely spot. At its center is Jacob Wrey Mould's spirited fountain of 1871, re-erected after years of

exile in the Bronx. The park also contains monuments to newspaper editor **Horace Greeley** (1890) by J. Q. A. Ward and the young Revolutionary War spy **Nathan Hale** (1893) by Frederick MacMonnies, installed close to the place where Hale was hanged by the British.

❼ City Hall Station

7

1900–4 · HEINS & LA FARGE

On October 27, 1904, the first segment of the Interborough Rapid Transit line (IRT) opened, running from City Hall to Grand Central Terminal and then up the west side under Broadway. The official dedication took place in the City Hall Station, planned from the start to be the showplace of the system. Guastavino tile vaults, elaborate colored mosaic work, stained-glass sky lights, handsome commemorative plaques, and suspended bronze chandeliers decorate the ticket lobby and the curving train platform.

The IRT system quickly outgrew the station; the platform's short length and tight curve could not accommodate the longer trains increasing ridership required. The station closed in December 1945, but its decoration is intact. The New York City Transit Museum offers tours by appointment.

Guastavino Tile

In 1885 the Spanish engineer Rafael Guastavino patented a system for constructing strong lightweight architectural vaults using overlapping and interlocking layers of thin terracotta tiles. His "Tile Arch System," an adaption of historic Spanish building practices, was quickly adopted by leading architects. They were attracted both by the system's ability to economically span large areas and by the elegant and distinctive appearance of Guastavino vaults. The engineer's work can also be seen at the Oyster Bar at Grand Central Terminal, the Registry Hall on Ellis Island, the crossing of the Cathedral of St. John the Divine, the arcade at the Municipal Building, and in the vaulted retail spaces under the approaches to the Queensborough Bridge.

❽ City Hall

1802–12 · JOSEPH FRANÇOIS
MANGIN AND JOHN MCCOMB JR.
WITH LATER ADDITIONS

City Hall was among New York's
tallest buildings at the time of its
completion. Today, surrounded
by larger and more imposing
structures, its delicacy and
restrained elegance are striking.
The building feels distinctly
French in its refined proportions,
carefully balanced plan, and
crisp detailing. At the same time
there is a relaxed openness
that is very much in tune with
the democratic ethos of Federal-
period America. Perhaps this
dual character is due to the
architects, one a French émigré,
the other native-born.

As seems nearly always to
be the case with civic buildings,
estimated construction costs
required some alterations
in Mangin and McComb's
original plans. To economize,
the specified marble for the rear facade was replaced with more
economical brownstone. The reasoning then was that since City Hall
was located at the northernmost boundry of the city, few people would
see it from the back.

The architectural focus of City Hall is the handsome central pavilion,
crowned by a cupola with a statue holding the scales of justice. Visitors
ascend a broad flight of steps leading to a columned porch, which
has long provided a dramatic setting for civic events. To the left and
right projecting wings bracket this ceremonial space.

Inside is a beautiful rotunda with a coffered dome and elegant
bronze railings. Over the years the building has been altered by a string
of architects, most notably by Grosvenor Atterbury, who in 1912 low-
ered the height of the dome and enlarged the oculus.

⊕ Chambers Street

❹ New York County ("Tweed") Courthouse

52 Chambers Street
1861–72 · JOHN KELLUM AND THOMAS LITTLE
1876–81 · LEOPOLD EIDLITZ

In New York the name of political boss William M. Tweed is synonymous with municipal corruption. The New York County Courthouse was Tweed's most egregious enterprise. The courthouse took nearly twenty years to complete and ended up costing in excess of $12 million; $9 million of that sum was graft.

Because the building took so long to construct, two architects were involved. The first, John Kellum, drew his inspiration from English Palladian precedents. Kellum's building, executed in stone, is symmetrically laid out. Two projecting wings flank a central portico and colossal pilasters march around the building and tie together the principal stories.

When architect Leopold Eidlitz took over in 1876, he changed stylistic gears. Eidlitz's south wing abandons classicism for the then-popular Victorian Romanesque.

Inside, Eidlitz added a bold and striking central rotunda. Under the influence of English critic John Ruskin, Eidlitz replaced encrusted monochromatic pilasters and pediments with richly colored structural brick and tile arches. The contrast between Kellum's lower floors and Eidlitz's above can be jarring, but it is an effective illustration of two schools of architectural thought.

McKim, Mead & White's majestic **Municipal Building** ❶ (1904–7) closes the vista at the end of the street. Behind a screen of Corinthian columns, the two curving wings draw us to a central triumphal arch. Across the way is the sumptuously Beaux-Arts **Surrogates Court/Hall of Records** ❸ (1899–1907) by John R. Thomas at 31 Chambers Street. The building's facade is enriched by fifty-four allegorial sculptures and depictions of important figures in the history of the city. Inside, the central marble atrium offers an elaborate double staircase and mosaics depicting the signs of the zodiac.

At Chambers Street, the character of Broadway shifts. From here up to Madison Square, Broadway is primarily a commercial corridor, and the surviving buildings are generally older than those farther south. There is also a new source of stylistic inspiration in evidence. Many of the buildings between City Hall and Houston Street were modelled on the palaces and civic buildings of sixteenth-century Italy. Some architects looked to Rome for inspiration, others to Florence, but the majority chose Venice as their source. Some buildings are near-literal copies of historic structures; in other cases, the inspiration is less specific.

This stretch of Broadway is also the center of the cast-iron district. Cast-iron facades enjoyed a great vogue in the middle years of the nineteenth century and offered developers significant advantages. Cast iron was lighter than stone and brick. It was strong, durable, easy to erect, and relatively fireproof. Unlike stone, where each block or panel needed to be individually carved, iron could be readily cast in elaborate designs. Modular sections could be mass produced, moved to the site and bolted together to create a facade. Where stone details can be softened and eroded by weather, cast iron, if properly maintained, never loses its crispness.

❾ Broadway Chambers Building

277 Broadway
1899–1900 · CASS GILBERT

This was Cass Gilbert's first
commission in New York. The
Broadway Chambers Building
is a three-part tower organized
along familiar lines, but Gilbert
has added a new twist: color. The
base is constructed of pinkish granite, the shaft of deep red and
blue brick, and the capital of red and yellow terra-cotta. Originally the
whole composition was topped by a green copper cornice, but this was
removed in 1925.

❿ A. T. Stewart Store
(later the Sun Building)

280 Broadway, NE corner of Chambers Street
1845–46 · JOSEPH TRENCH AND JOHN B. SNOOK
WITH LATER ADDITIONS

This imitation Renaissance palazzo, much expanded and altered over the years, was the home of New York's first department store. Built by one of the city's greatest and most innovative merchants, Alexander Turney Stewart, the store set a new standard for retail establishments. When completed, the gleaming marble facade stood out amid commercial buildings cheaply built of brick. Its Italianate style, inspired by the designs of mid-nineteenth-century London clubs, and its lavish interiors embodied elegance and sophistication.

So great was Stewart's success that in 1859, in need of more space, he moved his headquarters north to a new building at Broadway and Ninth Street. 280 Broadway was taken over by the *New York Sun* in 1919. A clock on Broadway, is a reminder that here at least *The Sun* never sets.

⓫ 287 Broadway

1871–72 · JOHN B. SNOOK

This is the first example we have encountered of a building with a cast-iron facade. There are many more in the blocks ahead, but the design of 287 Broadway is especially handsome.

Stylistically, 287 Broadway offers a glimpse of two moments in the evolution of taste. The Venetian-inspired design of the lower four stories, with their wide round-arched windows flanked by Corinthian columns, is typical of many cast-iron buildings of the 1850s and early 1860s. By the late 1860s, however, architectural fashion was shifting away from Italy toward Second Empire Paris. Snook responded by adding a French mansard roof with dormer windows at the top of his building.

In the next block, the east and west sides of Broadway are very different. On the west are two early twentieth-century office buildings designed with the familiar tripartite elevation. The **East River Savings Institution**, ⓬ (291 Broadway, 1910–11, Clinton & Russell), is dignified and conservative with a very nicely detailed four-story classical base. Next door, the **Barclay Building** ⓭ (303 Broadway, 1902, Stockton Colt) is even more conservative. A century later the postmodern mass of the **Ted Weiss Federal Building** ⓮ across the street (290 Broadway, 1994, Hellmuth, Obata, & Kassabaum) is hulking, anonymous, and bureaucratic. Much the same could be said for the **Javits Office Building** ⓕ that fills the next block, although the lobby does contain a colorful Sol Lewitt mural that looks particularly lively at night.

The Weiss Building contains the African Burial Ground National Monument, which marks the site of the nation's oldest and largest African-American cemetery. From the 1670s until 1794 this was the principal Manhattan burial place for both free and enslaved Africans in New York. The monument continues to the east on Duane Street with an outdoor memorial and park.

⓰ Mutual Reserve Building
(Langdon Building)

305 Broadway

1892–94 · WILLIAM H. HUME

The rough-hewn masonry, sturdy round arches, and thick walls ensure that this structure is firmly grounded. This is a building of granite and limestone, not cast iron or marble veneer. The motto of the original tenants, the Mutual Reserve Fund Life Association, was "Founded Upon a Rock." The building embraces the metaphor.

For all its emphasis on solidity, however, this is an elegantly detailed design. The columns flanking the windows in the central section facing Duane Street recede step by step into the depth of the wall. The foliate carving of the capitals of the main arcade vibrates with vitality. At the top story, the architect, instead of reducing the density of the stonework, added a powerful row of heavy squat arches with boldly rusticated voussoirs.

Farther west along Duane Street is a classic New York firehouse. The former home of **Fire Engine Company 7 and Hook and Ladder Company 1** ⓱ (100 Duane Street, 1904–5, Trowbridge & Livingston) sports a striped facade of alternating brick and limestone. With its bright red doors and trim, the design crackles with energy.

⓲ 319 Broadway

1869–70 · DAVID AND JOHN JARDINE

This building demonstrates the full potential of cast iron. The architect's inspiration came from sixteenth-century Venice, but this is not a dutiful copy of an historic palazzo. The design bursts with joyful confidence. There are large windows everywhere, flooding the interior with light. Those windows are set deeply into the facade, framed by receding arches supported by banded columns, each one topped with a richly detailed capital.

The wall's substantial depth catches the sun to create a clear and dramatic rhythm of light and shadow, accentuating the sculptural richness of the facade. The intermediate cornices between the floors (supported by Corinthian pilasters), along with the topmost cornice, enriched with delicate dentils and sturdy brackets, are all treated with similar boldness. Everything is carefully and masterfully balanced.

⓳ 8 Thomas Street
(David S. Brown Store)

1875–76 · J. MORGAN SLADE

Architect J. Morgan Slade drew his inspiration not from the Renaissance but from medieval Venice as interpreted in the writings of John Ruskin. High Victorian Gothic buildings based on his dictates abound in Britain. Few examples survive in twenty-first century New York, so 8 Thomas Street is a rarity.

The original cast-iron storefront is topped by four floors of diminishing height, each vigorously detailed in red brick

with contrasting stone arches, banded voussoirs, and highly polished granite columns. Although the basic vocabulary remains the same throughout, each floor has its own personality and rhythm. The tempo quickens as the building rises, culminating in the gable where a large oculus brings things to an emphatic stop.

⑳ 325 Broadway

1863–64

Here is another variation on the palazzo theme, this time built by real estate investor Henry Barclay. He leased the building to a number of dry-goods merchants who found their business thriving thanks to the increased demand for blankets and uniforms during the Civil War. Later, this building was home to the Remington Typewriter Company.

Unified behind a single facade, there are in fact three separate buildings here. The segmentally arched openings are carefully grouped and establish the plane of the exterior masonry wall. The large plate-glass windows themselves are recessed into the facade to establish a second taut and independent wall plane. The detailing is restrained and cleanly abstracted, with a distinct and original character. There are virtually no decorative flourishes.

㉑ New York Life Insurance Building

346 Broadway (108 Leonard St.)

1894–99 · STEPHEN D. HATCH WITH STANFORD WHITE OF McKIM, MEAD & WHITE

The New York Life Building is a large structure. Presenting a comparatively narrow face to Broadway, it stretches in a long trapezoid the full length of the block from Broadway to Lafayette Street between Catherine Lane and Leonard Street. The eastern portion of the building, designed by Hatch, was intended to join with an existing building on Broadway. Along the way the company changed plans, demolished the

old Broadway building and engaged the firm of McKim, Mead & White to extend and embellish Hatch's design for the full length of the block. The key feature of the new building was a tall tower pavilion on Broadway—a handsome accent and a nice trademark image for the company.

This is a building with two distinct parts. The bulk of the structure along Leonard Street is Hatch's work—a familiar Italian palazzo. The detailing here seems somewhat flat, timid, and monotonous. The narrow frontage on Broadway is occupied by McKim, Mead, & White's tower. The architectural vocabulary is essentially the same, but here the effect seems richer, fuller, and more assured. The fussy details of the older section are gone, replaced by deep rustication, bold cornices, sculptural bronze railings, and confidently applied classical decoration. At the top is a parapet crowned by stone eagles (the company's emblem) and by a distinctive tower housing a four-sided clock that still keeps time. By 1919 New York Life had outgrown 346

Broadway. In 1927 it moved into a new headquarters on Madison Square designed by Cass Gilbert. 346 Broadway is currently in the midst of conversion to high-end apartments, and the fate of some of its landmarked interiors is uncertain.

㉒ Thompson's Saloon

359 Broadway

1852 · FIELD & CORREJA

Between 1853 and 1859 the upper floors of 359 Broadway housed the sumptuously decorated studios of the celebrated photographer Matthew Brady. This was an essential stopping place for the rich, famous, and influential, all seeking a portrait likeness. If the prospect of the stairs or of a long posing session proved too daunting, clients could seek fortification at Thompson's Saloon on the ground floor. Today the building is certainly the worse for wear.

㉓ James S. White Building

361 Broadway

1881–82 · W. WHEELER SMITH

This unusually large cast-iron structure boasts two major facades, one on Broadway and the other on Franklin Street. The architect has taken full advantage of this substantial piece of real estate to lavish careful attention on his building's embellishment. Unlike many iron facades where window units were mass produced to an identical design, here

there is stunning variety. On each floor the corner piers display a different abstract floral or leaf pattern. The columns on each level are subtly varied as well, and the decoration of the pediment is particularly crisp.

❷❹ 366 Broadway
(Broadway-Franklin Building)

1907 · FREDERICK C. BROWNE

This is not an especially distinctive structure, but it features some wonderful, personality-filled caryatids and spirited decorative carving on the second level. The name of textile merchant and philanthropist Bernard Semel, a long-time occupant, still appears on the facade in bronze letters.

❷❺ 380 Broadway

1859

Here is an early example of a commercial building that features upper stories faced in marble above a cast-iron ground floor. The widely spaced arched windows retain their original two-over-two glazing. The center windows on the middle three floors are capped with handsome stone pediments, each one slightly different. The balance between glass and masonry here seems just about perfect. The arrangement of the fenestration on the White Street facade, on the other hand, has an appealingly quirky and syncopated rhythm.

Across the street the **Grosvenor Building** ㉖ at 385 Broadway (1875, Charles Wright) trumpets the names of its owners. Matilda Grosvenor and her sister Charlotte clearly understood the power of advertising when they added their name and the building's date to the prominent pediment that crowns the straightforward cast-iron facade.

388 Broadway ㉗ (1858, King & Kellum) and **400 Broadway** ㉘ (1862) present an interesting contrast in cast-iron design. **388** is light and open with tall, thin "sperm candle" columns, a term applied in the nineteenth century because the columns resembled slender candles made from sperm whale oil. Neighboring **400** is very much earthbound. Heavy rusticated quoins at each corner, flattened window arches, broad intermediate cornices, and a massive crowning pediment all contribute to the sense of weight and solidity. The upper sections of both facades look very much as if they are made of cast iron. In fact, they are stone.

At the intersection of Broadway and Canal Street is **415 Broadway** ㉙ (1927, Walker & Gillette). Built as the National City Bank, it was designed as a prototype for a series of new branch offices. It brings us into the twentieth century with its forthright, if stolid, art deco style.

Bleecker

Houston

Prince

Spring

Broadway

Greene

Mercer

Broome

Crosby

Grand

Howard

Canal

Lispenard

Walker

White

1. Arnold Constable and Company
2. Le Boutillier Brothers Store
3. 443 Broadway
4. 444 Broadway
5. D. Devlin and Co. Store
6. Mills & Gibb Building
7. 463 Broadway
8. Gila Building
9. Roosevelt Building
10. E. V. Haughwout and Company Store
11. Mechanics and Trader's Bank
12. Silk Exchange Building/Haggin Building
13. New Era Building
14. Loubat Stores
15. C. G. Gunther's Sons Store
16. De Forest Building
17. 529 Broadway
18. 537–541 Broadway
19. 540 Broadway
20. 542 Broadway
21. Charles Broadway Rouss Building
22. Scholastic Books
23. "Little" Singer Building
24. Rogers, Peet Store
25. 560 Broadway
26. Astor Building
27. 591–593 Broadway
28. Gateway Mural

Canal Street to Houston Street

Canal Street is the first of several major streets that cut all the way across Manhattan, their routes determined by natural geographic features. It takes its name from a drainage canal dug by the city in 1815 as part of the effort to fill in the Collect Pond. Once the chief source of water for Lower Manhattan, the Pond had become a foul dumping ground for garbage and dead animal carcasses, a perfect breeding ground for mosquitos, rodents, and disease. The Pond was filled in with dirt from Bayard Hill just to the north, then the highest spot in Lower Manhattan. To drain off the water, a canal was dug along a natural water course leading across the island through what were called the Lispenard Meadows. By 1820 the ditch had been covered over and became known as Canal Street.

Unfortunately, the drainage of the Collect Pond was not completely successful. The work was poorly carried out, and natural springs continued to make the area boggy. Soon the neighborhood north of City Hall and east of Broadway deteriorated into the Five Points slum. Broadway, however, was largely unaffected, and development pressed northward.

The section of Broadway from Canal Street to Astor Place, originally known as Great George Street, was laid out as early as 1775. It was renamed Broadway in 1794 and was fully paved by 1809, crossing the drainage canal on a wooden bridge. The neighborhood, particularly at its northern end, was initially residential. By 1850 it had developed into a fashionable shopping, entertainment, and hotel district. After the Civil War, the entertainment industry moved farther north, and the area became a center for the dry goods trade. The financial panic of 1873 slowed development, but by the late 1870s, large retail establishments, interspersed with warehouses and manufacturing businesses, were once again under construction.

By 1900 most of those retail businesses had once again moved on, and the area's economy switched to manufacturing. It was not until the 1960s that artists began to discover the neighborhood's wonderful stock of loft spaces. Galleries followed. Then, as artists and galleries were, in turn, priced out of the newly fashionable SoHo district, high-end shopping and luxury loft living took over.

From a walker's point of view, the greatest glory of SoHo is its cast-iron architecture. The twenty-six block SoHo Historic District has been described as the greatest assembly of cast-iron architecture anywhere. And while many of the best buildings are clustered on the side streets (particularly Greene and Broome), Broadway has more than its share.

As was the case to the south, most of these cast-iron facades drew their stylistic inspiration from Italian palazzo models. During the 1860s the impact of Second Empire Paris was also strongly in evidence. By the 1880s cast iron had begun to be replaced by brick and masonry designs, often with Queen Anne detailing. In the 1890s the impact of Beaux-Arts design principles and the development of steel-frame construction signaled another shift. Finally, around 1900 new building essentially came to a halt, to be revived only in the late twentieth century.

One block west of Broadway is a major retail monument:

❶ Arnold Constable and Company

307–11 Canal Street
1856

Aaron Arnold opened his first New York dry goods store in lower Manhattan in 1825. Thirty-two years later, he and his new partner

James Constable relocated to this building, soon dubbed "The Marble Palace." The marble half-palace would be more accurate. The main facade on Canal Street is dressed in the costly stone, but the side and rear elevations along Mercer and Howard Streets are in far more economical brick. High-end retailing has returned to the building in a clear sign that the neighborhood is changing.

❷ Le Boutillier Brothers Store

425 Broadway

1869 · GRIFFITH THOMAS

A.J. Ditenhoffer Warehouse

429 Broadway

1870–71 · THOMAS R. JACKSON

425 Broadway offers a modest cast-iron facade with square-headed windows framed by simple columns. The only extravagance is the cornice with its quirky broken pediment. The presence of a pedestal block under the break suggests the possibility of a missing statue.

429 Broadway is more ambitious. The cast-iron facade is ornamentally far richer: corner piers, columns, and spandrels are all handsomely decorated, and there is a fine pedimented cornice. Very few spaces are left unadorned. Yet the overall dignity and balance of the facade is never compromised. The secondary elevation along Howard Street is every bit as fully developed as that on Broadway, even though the ground floor arcade was disrupted by the later addition of a display window.

In the next block, **443 Broadway** ❸ (1860, Griffith Thomas) is an example of Thomas's earlier work. Here the classical facade is executed in stone rather than cast iron. The detailing is competent, if a bit awkward in its proportions. But the pediment above is as bold as the facade is reticent.

As you walk north, take a look

at architectural twins **444** and **452 Broadway** ❹ (1877). Note their distinctive cornice design and the lacy iron arches that frame the recessed windows, a motif imported from Second Empire Paris. Both buildings are the work of Schweitzer and Gruwé, who, copying Richard Morris Hunt's work at the Roosevelt Building in the next block, adopted these thin, flat screens as an alternative to the more sculptural treatment then popular for cast-iron facades in New York.

❺ D. Devlin and Co. Store

459–461 Broadway
1860–61

Dignified proportions, simple rhythmic round arches, and warm weathered stone give this structure real visual appeal. Three rusticated pavilions break up the long range of arches on the Grand Street elevation, much as the alternating bays do across the way at the Mills & Gibb Building.

❻ Mills & Gibb Building

462 Broadway
1879–80 · JOHN CORREJA

Built for a lace-and-linen import firm, this building is huge, extending east along Grand Street to Crosby Street. Straightforward and reductive, the design is relieved only by a few restrained decorative

touches, including 108 elegant Corinthian capitals on slender pilasters. The elements of the cast-iron facade have been kept as thin as possible to maximize the amount of glass admitting light into the interior.

Aware that the building's facade along Grand Street was extremely long, the architect broke it into bays to vary the rhythm of what might otherwise have been a monotonous parade of rectangular openings.

❼ 463 Broadway

2005–7 · JEAN NOUVEL WITH SLCE ARCHITECTS

The main block of this sleek and elegant building by French architect Jean Nouvel carefully maintains the existing roofline along Broadway. Floor heights and window proportions match those of the building's neighbors. The tower, set back from both Broadway and Grand Street, is designed to echo the slab of the Silk Exchange Building one block north on the corner of Broome Street.

Retail shops occupy the street level along both Broadway and Grand Street while high-end condominiums fill the rest of the building. These have a separate entrance around the corner at 40 Mercer Street. To ensure that all apartments receive ample natural light, the architect has devoted the northern quarter of the lot to a block-through courtyard visible through a glass wall on Broadway.

❽ Gila Building

472 Broadway
1878 · WILLIAM CAUVET

The Gila Building may be small, but it commands attention. The tall, skinny facade is topped with a dramatically raked and highly original cornice surmounted by a pair of improbably elongated urns. The architect also embellished the facade with a more elaborate version of the lacy iron screens on 444 and 452 Broadway and on the neighboring Roosevelt Building.

❾ Roosevelt Building

478, 480, 482 Broadway
1873–74 · RICHARD MORRIS HUNT

Commissioned by Roosevelt Hospital and constructed on the site of the house of its patron James Roosevelt, the Roosevelt Building is an early work by Richard Morris Hunt. The first American to study at the École des Beaux-Arts in Paris, Hunt is recognized for formalizing the profession in the United States and for his work for major public institutions, including the Metropolitan Museum of Art, as well as for titans of the Gilded Age, notably the Vanderbilt family.

The Roosevelt Building clearly reflects Hunt's studies in Europe. The center three stories of the elevation are linked by banded Ionic columns that support lacy metal segmental arches hovering in front of the main facade. At the top is a compositionally distinct attic story crowned by a very unusual cornice supported by thin pierced brackets. The building seems at once monumental and delicate.

The corner of Broadway and Broome Street is one of Manhattan's great architectural intersections.

⑩ E. V. Haughwout and Company Store

488–492 Broadway
1856–57 · JOHN P. GAYNOR
CAST-IRON FACADE BY DANIEL D. BADGER

It would be hard to imagine a more visually satisfying building. Each detail is carefully considered on its own, and everything works together to create a majestic and dignified composition that anchors the street corner and lends distinction to the entire neighborhood.

Gaynor's inspiration was the famous library in St. Mark's Square in Venice by the Renaissance architect Jacopo Sansovino. Instead of stone, here the material is cast iron, fabricated by the founder Daniel D. Badger, who supplied iron for more than 500 buildings over the course of his career in locations from New York to Cairo.

Sansovino's library is two stories tall; Badger and Gaynor expanded

ttheir design to five. They compressed the elements slightly, reduced the amount of decorative detail, increased the depth of the facade, and separated each story with a strong cornice, to create a composition of intensity and dignity. The crisp detailing further ensures that the building crackles with energy. Unlike Sansovino's building, which dissolves into the sky through a balustrade and a row of statuary, the Haughwout store is contained by a projecting cornice that adds to the design's compact power.

The building was commissioned by merchant Eder V. Haughwout to house his fashionable emporium for cut glass, silver, china, clocks, chandeliers, and the like. The Lincolns bought their White House dinner service here. The store also boasted the first hydraulic passenger elevator in New York.

⑪ Mechanics and Traders Bank

486 Broadway

1882–85 · LAMB & RICH

Here is another building that presents a narrow facade to Broadway (so it could claim the coveted address) with the main structure extending down the side street where real estate was less expensive. In this case, the Broome Street elevation is by far the more interesting. The architects have worked up a composition in which two rich red-brick towers flank a section of dark green cast-iron infill. The mansard roof of the center section and some light Queen Anne detailing provide an appealing contrast to the bulky solidity of the towers.

⑫ Silk Exchange Building/ Haggin Building

487 Broadway

1894–95 · JOHN T. WILLIAMS

A commercial extravaganza, this building stretches the entire length of the block from Broadway to Mercer Street. The great thin slab would have been a challenge to build in the era before steel-frame

12

construction. Here that frame supports a sturdy stone-clad base. The seven-story central section in buff brick is articulated by colossal pilasters and thermal windows. The richest embellishment, in terra-cotta, fills the spandrels and virtually every inch of the attic floors. The composition is topped off with a powerful copper-clad cornice.

⓭ New Era Building

495 Broadway

1896–97 · BUCHMAN & DEISLER

Squat, muscular columns support
a five-story central section topped
by three exuberantly decorated
arches. The composition is
crowned with a splendid copper-
clad mansard, pierced by
stacked dormers. The small-pane
fenestration is a nice touch,
as are the flattened balconies
beneath each window, adapted
from Italian Renaissance *cantorie*. Originally the home of a printing
company, the building was later the headquarters of Butler Brothers,
America's first mail-order catalogue company.

⓮ Loubat Stores

503–511 Broadway

1878–79 · JOHN B. SNOOK

Here are three linked buildings,
built by the same architect for
the same patron. The Loubat
Stores are dignified and
straightforward, even a bit
austere. The unusual cornice
adds just the right amount of
distinctive personality.

⓯ C. G. Gunther's Sons Store

502 Broadway

1860 · JOHN KELLUM AND SON

Here's a lively facade with classic
tall "sperm candle" columns.

Such columns are applied regularly on cast-iron facades in Lower Manhattan, but seldom are they handled with such assurance. Only the ground floor is iron; the upper stories are executed in stone.

⑯ De Forest Building

513–517 Broadway
1884 · LAMB & RICH

Another sober, luxurious composition from Lamb & Rich—deep red brick, green-painted iron, and fine decorative terra-cotta.

Broome Street and LOMEX

During the 1940s New York City Planning Commissioner and building czar Robert Moses proposed the construction of a ten-lane elevated expressway across Lower Manhattan to link the Holland Tunnel with the Williamsburg and Manhattan Bridges. LOMEX, as the project was known, would have required the demolition of fourteen blocks of historic buildings in Soho and Little Italy and relocation of more than 2,000 families. The project was ultimately defeated in the 1960s, thanks in good part to the efforts of activist Jane Jacobs and the local community.

⓱ 529 Broadway

2016 · BKSK ARCHITECTS

A sympathetic contemporary building in steel, glass, and coppery terra-cotta, topped off with a projecting cornice. The Broadway front responds to the gridded cast-iron facades of its neighbors, while terra-cotta dominates the Spring Street elevation. The lower lintels twist, drop, and ultimately flatten as they follow the slope of Spring Street.

⓲ 537–541 Broadway

1868—69 · CHARLES METTAM

The middle three floors of this vigorous and satisfying cast-iron design feature shallow flattened arcades, the arches springing from barely engaged columns with crisply detailed capitals. At the cornice level there are three separate pediments, one triangular, two segmentally curved. Jaunty finial urns punctuate the composition.

⓳ 540 Broadway

1867 · DAVID & JOHN JARDINE

Everything here is flat and planar, rather than round and sculptural, but the assured energy is real. Notice the incised, banded, and interlaced decoration around the windows and the way the

abstracted fleur-de-lis carving on the lower floors gives way at the cornice to a pediment bearing the building's date. Clearly careful attention was paid to the elevation and detailing, but the dour ashen color of the stone does not work in the building's favor.

⑳ 542 Broadway

1864

Three Grecian goddesses preside from the top floor. They represent Panaceia, the goddess of healing, Athena, goddess of wisdom, and Ceres, goddess of agriculture and fertility. They were added in 1897 in a likely effort to add distinction to an otherwise ordinary commercial loft building.

㉑ Charles Broadway Rouss Building

555 Broadway

1889–90 · ALFRED ZUCKER

Charles Rouss came to New York after the Civil War penniless. He made millions in the retail trade and was proud of it. To celebrate, he adopted Broadway as his middle name and splashed it across the front of his store. As if that were not enough, a decade later he added an elaborate cornice and pyramidal dormers incorporating his name along with the

building's date. In 1906 Rouss's
son erected an annex store,
also emblazoned with his
father's name, around the corner
at 123-5 Mercer Street. His
plan to connect the two stores
with a tunnel for shoppers was
never realized.

㉒ Scholastic Books

557 Broadway
2001 · ALDO ROSSI AND
GENSLER ASSOCIATES

This is Italian architect Aldo
Rossi's only building in New York.
Clearly Rossi and his associates
worked hard to respect the
character of the neighborhood.
The fenestration and the
cornices line up with the adjacent
buildings and the facade was
assembled like older cast iron
buildings from modular parts, but

the over-scaled white concrete columns seem too insistent. It's worth
a walk around the corner to see the rear facade on Mercer Street. Here
monumental flat steel arches are bolted together in a bold embrace
of the utilitarian. The color scheme—dull red and pale green—echoes
that of the neighboring Little Singer Building.

㉓ "Little" Singer Building

561 Broadway
1902–4 · ERNEST FLAGG

Like most designs of Ernest Flagg, this facade rewards scrutiny.
Sparkling glass, rich red terra-cotta panels (some plain, some
decorated), and an elegant green steel screen all combine into a
glorious overall composition. The building is a large one (there is
another facade on Prince Street), but it is wonderfully airy and light.

Take some time to enjoy the abstracted steel Ionic columns at the third level, the glass and steel awning, and the energetic scrolling of the screen spandrels. All the details convey controlled exuberance and great finesse.

Singer's larger original headquarters was one of New York's great early skyscrapers. It once stood at the corner of Broadway and Liberty Street, but it was demolished in 1968.

㉔ Rogers, Peet Store

575 Broadway
1881–82 · THOMAS STENT

Stent's solid and imposing structure features some inventive Victorian detailing. Notice, for example, the deeply set segmental arched windows on the fifth level with their small flanking columns. Each level is distinct and offers something interesting to discover. The cast-iron storefront at ground level is splendid in its abstract precision.

Rogers, Peet moved here from their prior home on Broadway opposite City Hall in 1882. The clothier departed in 1902, and the lower floors of the building have been substantially

remodeled twice at the turn of the twenty-first century. In 1996 Arata Isozaki turned it into a short-lived home for a branch of the Guggenheim Museum. Then in 2001 Rem Koolhaas arrived to create the current dramatic multilevel interior with its wave-like floor for Prada.

㉕ 560 Broadway

1883–84 · THOMAS STENT

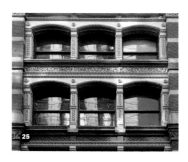

The Rogers, Peet Store is a meditation on the possibilities of brick. Here, at least on the Broadway facade, Stent has shifted the visual balance. Now there is plenty of stone, much of it carved. The effect is simultaneously lighter and fussier than the facade across the street. 560 Broadway has presence and dignity, but it seems a little timid by comparison. Along Prince Street, the stone disappears, replaced by more economical brick on this secondary facade.

Much of the land in this neighborhood, including both 560 and 575 Broadway, was developed by the Astors, one of Manhattan's great land-owning families. For a time, Stent was their favored architect. As architectural tastes evolved in the 1890s, they moved on to other designers.

㉖ Astor Building

583 Broadway

1896–97 · CLEVERDON & PUTZEL

The Astors must have been pleased by this turn-of-the-century office building in grand style. The facade is fully expressed with thick stone walls and beautifully executed classical detailing. Above the arcaded ground level, monumental Corinthian columns flank reentrant windows and support a strong, projecting entablature. The lush carving here is mirrored by an equally confident composition at the top of the building. In between, the restrained middle stories provide a visual respite that heightens the impact of the embellishment above and below.

㉗ 591–593 Broadway

1860

These two buildings once shared a common facade design, still visible in the cast-iron shop fronts at the ground level. Around 1900, the upper floors of 591 Broadway were remodeled in brick and terra-cotta. The top story with its Flemish Renaissance gable is quite distinctive.

As a conclusion to this walk, take a moment to look at Forrest Myers's mural *The Gateway to Soho* ㉘ on the southwest corner of Broadway and Houston Street. A pioneering work of public art, it was originally installed in 1973. In 2007, to free up additional space for advertising as the neighborhood re-emerged as a major retail center, the mural was repositioned higher on the wall.

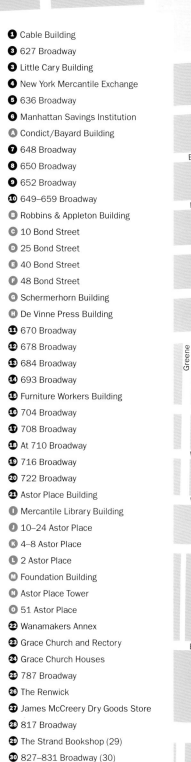

1. Cable Building
2. 627 Broadway
3. Little Cary Building
4. New York Mercantile Exchange
5. 636 Broadway
6. Manhattan Savings Institution
A. Condict/Bayard Building
7. 648 Broadway
8. 650 Broadway
9. 652 Broadway
10. 649–659 Broadway
B. Robbins & Appleton Building
C. 10 Bond Street
D. 25 Bond Street
E. 40 Bond Street
F. 48 Bond Street
G. Schermerhorn Building
H. De Vinne Press Building
11. 670 Broadway
12. 678 Broadway
13. 684 Broadway
14. 693 Broadway
15. Furniture Workers Building
16. 704 Broadway
17. 708 Broadway
18. At 710 Broadway
19. 716 Broadway
20. 722 Broadway
21. Astor Place Building
I. Mercantile Library Building
J. 10–24 Astor Place
K. 4–8 Astor Place
L. 2 Astor Place
M. Foundation Building
N. Astor Place Tower
O. 51 Astor Place
22. Wanamakers Annex
23. Grace Church and Rectory
24. Grace Church Houses
25. 787 Broadway
26. The Renwick
27. James McCreery Dry Goods Store
28. 817 Broadway
29. The Strand Bookshop (29)
30. 827–831 Broadway (30)
31. 836 Broadway (31)
32. Roosevelt Building

Houston Street to 14th Street

This is the spot where the Commissioners' 1811 plan for Manhattan's street grid was supposed to start. (It actually gets fully underway farther north at Thirteenth Street.) Today Houston Street is a major traffic way, but this was not always the case. Its present boulevard-like dimensions were established in the 1930s when the street was widened to accommodate the new IND subway line beneath. Even today, there are empty lots, exposed rear building elevations, and a somewhat raggedy streetscape left from the demolition.

Like so much of Manhattan, the blocks north of Houston Street were initially farmland. During the 1830s and 1840s, the areas around Astor Place and Grace Church had become prime residential territory. Theaters and hotels quickly followed. In 1862 A. T. Stewart opened a huge retail store at Broadway and Ninth Street. From this point until about 1910, the area from Houston to Fourteenth Street was a major retail center. Because new buildings were designed not only as spaces to store and process goods but also as venues for their sale, they needed to be architecturally impressive to attract shoppers.

The streetscape along Broadway from Houston Street to Astor Place is remarkably uniform in style. Many of the buildings were constructed during the prosperous 1880s. The financial panic of 1893 brought development to a temporary halt, but building resumed just after the turn of the century. A major catalyst was the construction of Wannamaker's annex, which fills the entire block on the east side of Broadway between Ninth and Tenth Streets.

In the early twentieth century, neither the arrival of Wannamaker's, nor the opening of the IRT subway under Lafayette Street in 1904, nor even the completion of the BMT subway along Broadway itself in 1917 could stem the northward migration of department stores away from what is now called NoHo. This stretch of Broadway entered a long period of decline; little new was built until the 1960s when New York University began a major campus expansion.

❶ Cable Building

611 Broadway

1892–94 · MCKIM, MEAD & WHITE

Until 1917, when the BMT subway opened, travelers along Broadway relied mostly on horse-drawn omnibus service. In 1892 a supplemental cable-car line opened, extending from the Battery to 50th Street. The aptly named Cable Building was the headquarters of its operator, the Metropolitan Traction Company. The firm gave their architects a challenge: design a building of aesthetic distinction to house not only the company's offices but also its powerhouse. 611 Broadway was McKim, Mead & White's response. The upper floors were devoted to offices. Down below in a cavernous basement were massive steam engines and the thirty-two-foot winding wheels that drove the cable through its slots under Broadway. The cable traction system could move cars at up to thirty miles per hour, but it was plagued from the start with problems. In 1901 it was replaced by electrically powered cars. Today the basement space that once housed the winding machinery is occupied by the Angelika Film Center.

On the facade, the variegated buff-colored roman bricks, crisp terra-cotta classical ornament, and handsome copper cornice are characteristic of McKim, Mead & White's polished style. Industrial details around the windows reflect the use of the building; an oval window and flanking figures by sculptor J. Massey Rhind mark the entrance.

➋ 627 Broadway

(NoHo Building)

1894 · LOUIS KORN

The tripartite elevation of the NoHo Building echoes that of the Cable Building, but here the classical detailing is restrained and abstracted. The exception is the rich terra-cotta work around the upper three stories.

➌ Little Cary Building

620 Broadway

1858–59 · JOHN B. SNOOK

CAST-IRON FACADE DANIEL D. BADGER

These handsome stacked classical arches flanked by paired columns were all executed in cast iron by the firm of Daniel D. Badger and Company. The simulated rustication of the wall surface is distinctive, contrasting as it does with the delicacy of the fluting on the columns. The current cream-and-blue color scheme accentuates the deep window reveals and gives the building a striking plasticity.

The building name is somewhat misleading. The "Big" Cary Building (1856) is downtown at 105 Chambers Street. Different patron, different architect, but the cast-iron facade was assembled from identical components supplied by the Badger firm.

❹ New York Mercantile Exchange

628 Broadway

1882 · HERMAN J. SCHWARZMANN WITH BUCHMAN & DEISLER

628 Broadway housed the back offices of the main Mercantile Exchange downtown on Harrison Street, but the owners did not miss the opportunity to advertise their firm. They emblazoned its name across the banded courses of the nearly flat cast-iron facade. That otherwise plain elevation is enlivened with filigree and plant-inspired decoration. The lily bouquets and engaged colonettes with their stalks of bamboo are particularly appealing.

❺ 636 Broadway

1896 · GEORGE B. POST

This is the first of several buildings we will encounter by the prolific George B. Post. Nearly all employ the same effective compositional formula: a two-story base, a tall central section linked by an arcade of colossal pilasters or half columns, and an attic story and cornice. Here those impressive engaged

columns, handsomely banded with terra-cotta, are constructed of frankly exposed brick. The top two stories were added in 1905.

❻ Manhattan Savings Institution Building

644 Broadway

1889–90 · STEPHEN D. HATCH

This richly colored confection of sandstone, brick, terra-cotta, and cast iron dominates the intersection of Broadway and Bleecker Street. Above the solid, rusticated Romanesque base, the style switches to a delicate Queen Anne. The upper stories culminate in a copper-clad turret surmounting the chamfered corner.

Louis Sullivan

Ⓐ Condict/Bayard Building

65 Bleecker Street

1897–99 · LOUIS SULLIVAN

Louis Sullivan believed that the facades of tall buildings should proudly express not only their height, but the presence underneath of the steel structure that supports the building. He also believed that since the skyscraper was a new building type without historic precedent, it required a new decorative vocabulary that did not rely on recycled historical motifs.

Abandoning the three-part column model of base, shaft, and capital, Sullivan's Bayard Building rises unimpeded from the ground floor to the cornice. There is a thrilling expression of verticality in the piers that run the full height of the building, unbroken by intermediate horizontal courses. At their apex the piers terminate in a row of interlocking large and small arches. In the spandrels the architect placed a band of willowy angels with outspread wings. Finally, there is a boldly projecting cornice with decorative cresting and a lushly carved soffit.

At every level Sullivan provided terra-cotta embellishment—rich, dense, and bursting with organic energy.

No single building on the east side of Broadway between Bleecker and Bond Streets is especially distinguished, yet as an ensemble they encapsulate the history of Broadway's architectural evolution in the second half of the nineteenth century.

Next door to the Manhattan Savings Institution, **648 Broadway** ❼ (1891, Cleverdon & Putzel) shares a similar boldness in its decorative vocabulary. Notice in particular the willful awkwardness of the two-story addition tacked onto the roof in 1898. As you pass **650 Broadway** ❽ (1860) you can observe the simpler, flatter, more restrained preferences of an earlier generation.

652 Broadway ❾ (1906, Frederick C. Browne) is poised and urbane. A two-story metal shop window is surmounted by a large scrolling stone keystone and a small aedicula. Then comes a middle section of grouped windows in a recessed metal bay under a segmental arch, and finally a row of Doric columns leading to a prominent cornice. The French-inflected elevation was a popular one for commercial buildings in turn-of-the-century New York. Browne will use it again a few blocks farther north.

Across the street at **649–659 Broadway** ❿ is a group of four closely related buildings erected between 1866 and 1883, originally to designs by Griffith Thomas and Henry Fernbach. During the 1870s this was the home of celebrated carpet merchants W. & J. Sloane. In 1979 a fire caused serious damage to the buildings. The exuberant facades above the generic modern arcade on the ground floor are largely reconstructions.

⇨ Bond Street/ Lafayette Street

Bond Street between Broadway and Bowery epitomizes the multi-faceted streetscape of Manhattan, with its cobbled street and contemporary buildings interspersed among the nineteenth-century lofts.

Ⓑ Robbins & Appleton Building

1-5 Bond Street

1879-80 · STEPHEN D. HATCH

Here is another gem by Stephen Hatch. The material is cast iron, and the stylistic inspiration comes from Second Empire Paris. Under a mansard roof with multiple dormers, the architect marshals rows of deeply set windows and acres of glass between distinct cornices. This confident and appealing structure demands our attention.

Ⓒ 10 Bond Street

2014 · SELLDORF ARCHITECTS

This richly hued luxury co-op apartment building in steel and terra-cotta is the perfect bookend to the Brooks Brothers Building at the west end of the block. Nearly a century and a half separate the buildings, yet both share the same lush coloring, bold detailing, and architectural confidence. Note the interesting pergola at the top, added at the request of the Landmarks Commission to bring the building's height into closer conformity with its neighbors.

Walking east, there are more contemporary residential buildings in the next block: **25 Bond Street** ❶ (2008, BKSK), **40 Bond Street** ❷ (2008, Herzog & de Meuron), **48 Bond Street** ❸ (2008, Deborah Berke).

Walking north on Lafayette, there are two major landmarks.

❼ Schermerhorn Building

376–380 Lafayette Street

1888–89 · HENRY J. HARDENBERGH

Hardenbergh, architect of the Plaza Hotel and Dakota Apartments, offers us a symphony of carefully calibrated colors and materials: buff and red brick, polished granite, carved brownstone, terra-cotta, and copper. The facade rises from squat, engaged granite columns, doubled at the corner. These support an arcade of segmental arches that give way to three stories of beautifully laid red brick, topped by another row

of segmental arches. Here the color scheme shifts to buff, lightening the appearance of the upper floors, before the facade terminates in a dark stone cornice. The cast decoration on the buttresses and the carved heads topping the pilasters higher up are beautifully done.

Don't miss the calculated asymmetry of the two corner service towers that flank the main block—one on Great Jones Street and one on Lafayette. They are among the most freely inventive components of the design.

376 Lafayette Street was built by William C. Schermerhorn on the site of his family home. The Schermerhorns, an old Knickerbocker clan, owned large parcels of Manhattan real estate. Perhaps the most well-known member of the family was Caroline Schermerhorn, who married William Backhouse Astor Jr. to become "The Mrs. Astor" of New York 400 fame.

ⓗ De Vinne Press Building

393–99 Lafayette Street

1885–86 · BABB, COOK & WILLARD

The De Vinne Press Building is massive with thick load-bearing walls,
yet the effect is taut, smooth, and elegant. Seldom has brick been
employed with greater finesse. Some of the windows are flush with the
facade, others are deeply recessed. The size and placement of these
openings has been flawlessly calculated to produce a finely balanced
overall composition. At the corner, brick quoins accent the softly
rounded transition from one facade to the other. Looking up, notice how
the slightly pitched roof facing Lafayette Street flattens at the corner
to make the shift to the running cornice along East Fourth Street.
Finally, don't miss the understated main portal with its fine latticed
wrought iron gate and pierced terra-cotta frame. 393 Lafayette was
built by Theodore De Vinne, a printer with a reputation for elegant
and meticulous work. The building reflects his passion for perfection.

⓫ 670 Broadway
(Brooks Brothers Store)

1873–74 · GEORGE E. HARNEY

The fourth home of the famous men's clothier Brooks Brothers (established in 1818) is muscular and assertive. Dark red brick is set off by hard white stone and enlivened with bold decorative flourishes. On the Broadway side, the numbers in the ornamental iron tie plates give the building's date. The smooth stone trim is incised with crisp floral and geometric decorations, and the stone column capitals are beautifully carved. Note the angular saw-tooth cutting on the second-floor arches, the vigorously patterned brickwork, and a crisp corbel table that merges seamlessly into the cornice. At street level the cast iron columns have quirky capitals and slightly threatening claw-like bases.

⓬ 678 Broadway

1874 · DAVID & JOHN JARDINE

This cast-iron facade is two doors up from Brooks Brothers and dates from about the same year. Where Brooks Brothers is bold and assertive from the ground up, here the elevation gains momentum as it rises. The lower floors are comparatively shallow in relief and generic in conception, but at the top level, the windows are deeply set and the decorative elements are emphatically sculptural. The size of the projecting cornice, in fact, makes the building look a little top heavy. Notice the difference in scale between that powerful cornice and the delicate sunburst motif placed over each top-floor window. The design was likely assembled from pre-made parts.

⓭ 684 Broadway

1905 · FREDERICK C. BROWNE

The basic design formula of 652 Broadway is applied here, but this time the patron had more money. Everything is bolder, fuller, and

more vigorous. The star attraction is the pair of lions heads under the cornice. More animals appear nearby at **693 Broadway** ⓐ (1908, William C. Frohne) where some very stern owls peer down from the fourth-floor cornice.

⓯ Furniture Workers Building

700 Broadway
1890 · GEORGE B. POST

Here Post employs the colossal brick pilasters of 636 Broadway to a prominent corner site. The

effect here is richer and more plastic. There is fine brickwork, strong terra-cotta, and at the cornice line, an appealing row of gargoyles. If you notice a family resemblance between this and the Schermerhorn Building, it is probably not a coincidence. The architect is different, but the patron, the Schermerhorn family, and the aesthetic are the same.

The rest of the block offers a pleasing and varied sequence of commercial loft buildings from the 1890s. Next door at **704 Broadway** ⓰ (1894–95, DeLemos & Cordes) there is a wealth of Renaissance-inspired

detail to discover on a somewhat disjointed facade that would certainly look more pulled together if it hadn't lost its cornice. **708 Broadway** ⓱ (1896, Cleverdon & Putzel) is a similar composition, inflected this time by northern European rather than Italian Renaissance models.

At **710 Broadway** ⓲ (1894, Cleverdon & Putzel) the architects have designed something more densely textured and quirky. The stacked terra-cotta friezes, cornices, and finials are energetic and spirited. A little further down the block, take a look at the very top of the strikingly red **716 Broadway** ❶❾ (1889, Alfred Zucker) for a pair of watchful gargoyles. Fans of architectural sculpture should also look up at the **Keller Building, 722 Broadway** ❷⓿ (1895) by German architect Francis A. Minuth for a row of vigorously carved grotesque heads, wreaths, and lions.

❷❶ Astor Place Building
(One Astor Place)

750 Broadway

1881 · STARKWEATHER & GIBBS

The Astor Place Building was originally designed as a hotel and boarding house, but it was soon converted to manufacturing use. The building was commissioned by prominent politician and developer Orlando Potter, who hired the same architect to design the Potter Building on Park Row a year later.

This was clearly intended to be a luxurious building. The first floor is cast iron enriched by neo-Grec details. Above, the material shifts to red brick with brown terra-cotta trim. Each floor has its own personality. The deeply set windows are accented by an array of different sills and moldings and enlivened by an imaginative variety of heads, capitals, corbels, and decorative panels.

⬦ Astor Place

Down the block at 13–25 Astor Place is the **Mercantile Library Building** ❶ (1890, George E. Harney), a handsome, understated brick and terra-cotta endeavor. The library was founded in 1820 for the benefit of working men. Its goal was to distract them through reading from less wholesome entertainment. In 1890 the Library boasted 12,000 members and a collection of 120,000 volumes.

The entire south side of Astor Place also owes its development to Orlando Potter. He began at the east end of the block in 1875 with **10–24 Astor Place** ❿, designed by Griffith Thomas in a striking combination of brick, stone, and cast iron. Midblock **4–8 Astor Place** Ⓚ (1891) is the work of architect Francis H. Kimball. The more imposing **2 Astor Place** Ⓛ (740-744 Broadway) on the corner dates to 1910 and is also by Kimball.

Closing the view to the east is the venerable **Foundation Building** Ⓜ of The Cooper Union for the Advancement of Science and Art (1853–59, Frederick A. Peterson), with **Astor Place Tower** Ⓝ (2005, Gwathmey Siegel) to the south and **51 Astor Place** Ⓞ (2013, Fumihiko Maki) to the north.

❷❷ Wanamakers Department Store Annex

756–770 Broadway

1904–10 AND 1926 · D.H. BURNHAM & COMPANY

The story of this block-filling monolith began in 1848 at Broadway and Chambers Street when A. T. Stewart opened his celebrated department store. By 1862 Stewart had outgrown his Marble Palace and moved north, constructing a new six-story cast-iron emporium filling the entire block along the east side of Broadway between Ninth and Tenth Streets: the Iron Palace. The new Stewart store was a retail landmark that marked the beginning of the Ladies Mile.

After Stewart's death in 1876 the business declined, and in 1896 it was taken over by Philadelphia merchant John Wanamaker. Like his predecessor, Wanamaker was ambitious. In 1903 he commissioned Chicago architect Daniel Burnham to design a twelve-story annex filling the whole block to the south.

Burnham connected the Iron Palace to his Renaissance-style annex with a pedestrian bridge across Ninth Street ("The Bridge of Progress"). Inside, an enormous sky-lit rotunda filled the center of the new store. In addition to selling just about any type of merchandise imaginable, there were restaurants, retiring rooms, a theater seating 1,300, and a formidable organ with 7,422 pipes.

22

Wanamakers continued in business until 1954, when the store closed. As for the original Iron Palace, it burned to the ground in 1956. A generic white-brick apartment building now fills the entire site.

At Tenth Street, Broadway, which has run straight as an arrow northward from Bowling Green, now angles to the west. This shift created the prominent building site elegantly occupied by Grace Church. If you look south, the end of your view is filled by the spire of the Woolworth Building. Grace Church and the "Cathedral of Commerce" are serendipitous Gothic bookends for this mile-and-a-half-long stretch of Broadway.

There is an ongoing debate as to why Broadway makes a turn at this point. Some ascribe it to the refusal of Henry Brevoort, who owned a farm here, to allow the City Commissioners to impose their street grid on his property. Others suggest that the re-routing was undertaken to align Broadway more closely with the Bowery to permit a smoother meeting of these two important thoroughfares in the blocks ahead. In any case, politics, money, and real estate interests were all certainly involved.

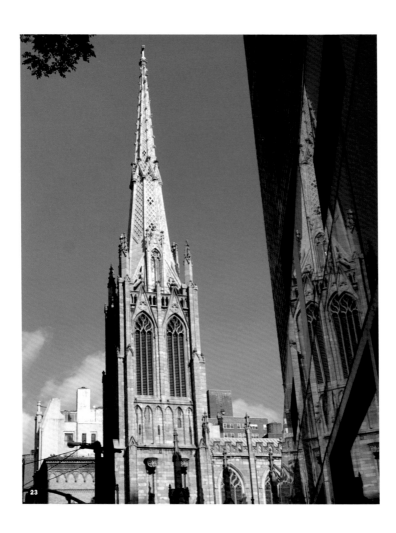

23

➋➌ Grace Church and Rectory

800 and 804 Broadway
1843–46, JAMES RENWICK JR.

1846 was a great year for the Gothic style in New York: both Grace and Trinity Churches opened their new buildings. Grace Church was founded in 1808, directly across the street from Trinity. In 1843, in need of additional room, Grace Church looked northward and built a new sanctuary on the present site.

They chose James Renwick Jr., a twenty-four-year-old engineer, as their architect. This commission launched a career that was later to include such landmarks as the Smithsonian's Castle in Washington, D.C., and St. Patrick's Cathedral on Fifth Avenue.

Both Trinity and Grace are essentially English parish churches, albeit lavish ones. Each has a long central nave and two aisles, a central entry tower, and a deep chancel. Renwick's innovation at Grace Church was to add transepts to the north and south of the nave.

Downtown at Trinity, Richard Upjohn used sandstone as his material, giving the church a quiet, recessive character. At Grace Church, Renwick chose white Tuckahoe marble—quarried by convicts doing hard labor at Sing Sing prison. The same marble was used forty years later when, in 1881, the original wooden steeple was replaced by Upjohn's dramatic and crisply detailed stone spire.

In 1878 Edward T. Potter built the Chantry Chapel to the south side of the church. The materials are the same, but the design displays a High Victorian sensibility. The composition is compressed and slightly edgy, with a concentrated energy. The decorative elements (buttresses, crockets, portal sculpture, balusters, etc.) are packed closely together in contrast to the more relaxed and expansive posture of Renwick's main church.

Inside the church, a broad nave with intricate lierne vaulting is flanked by two aisles and terminates in a dramatic east window behind the lavishly decorated altar. The east window, by the prominent English firm of Clayton and Bell, was installed in 1878 at the same time as the altar. Like the Chantry Chapel, the altar reflects the influence of English High Victorian taste in its detailing, rich polychromy, and sumptuous materials. The aisle windows, many designed by Englishman Henry Holiday, are interesting for their Pre-Raphaelite style.

Before leaving the church, don't miss the beautifully carved portals in the north and south transepts, the baptismal font surrounded by mosaics, or the wooden pulpit. The box pews survive from the nineteenth century. A bust of Renwick is installed in the west corner of the north transept.

On the north side of the church is the picturesque rectory, set back from the sidewalk by a quiet garden. It bristles with oriel windows, buttresses, finials, flamboyant tracery, and all manner of Gothic decorative detailing. The large urn in front is a Roman antiquity, the gift of a parishioner to an early Rector.

Behind the church, on Fourth Avenue, is the rest of the Grace Church campus.

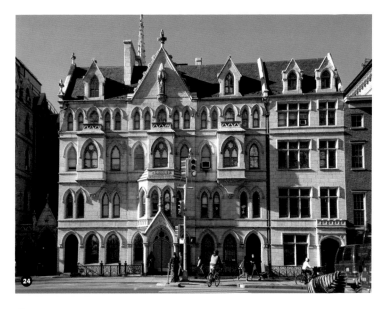

㉔ Grace Church Houses

92–98 Fourth Avenue

1892 · HEINS & LA FARGE (92)
1883 · JAMES RENWICK JR. (94–96)
1907 · RENWICK, ASPINWALL & TUCKER (98)

These three distinct but stylistically related buildings were originally intended for clergy housing, for community outreach, and for a choir school. Take a moment to compare Renwick's central building of 1883

with the later structures to either side. Taken together they neatly illustrate the evolution of Gothic Revival architecture in the later nineteenth century.

The complex, which now houses the Grace Church School, was very nearly demolished in the 1970s, but it was saved in an early instance of citizen-driven architectural preservation.

In deference to Grace Church, the designers of the apartment house across the street at **787 Broadway** ㉕ added a few generic Gothic touches to an otherwise unremarkable twentieth-century building. On the east side, **The Renwick** ㉖ at 808 Broadway (1887-88; Renwick, Aspinwall & Russell) is far more rewarding. Designed in buff brick and terra-cotta, a toned-down Gothic vocabulary is applied to what was originally a commercial building. The ivy-covered south wall presents an appealingly asymmetrical and understated face to the rectory garden.

㉗ James McCreery Dry Goods Store

67 East 11th Street
1868-70 · JOHN KELLUM

At the McCreery store, the rhythmic march of round Italianate arches wraps around the corner and then appears to extend almost without end down 11th Street.

McCreery was a retail pioneer in this neighborhood, establishing his store here in 1868, a few years after A. T. Stewart's Iron Palace. In 1894, following fashion, he moved his emporium uptown. The Broadway building subsequently housed a number of businesses and workshops until a fire in 1971 reduced it to a shell. Happily, the cast-iron facade survived. Thanks to community effort, that shell was retained and a new apartment building erected behind it. While the Second-Empire mansard that so magnificently crowned the original building has been replaced by a plain two-story attic, the survival of the rest of the facade is cause for celebration.

㉘ 817 Broadway

1895 · GEORGE B. POST

This handsome building is executed in beautifully laid Roman brick and fine terra-cotta. Here Post's characteristic colossal pilasters rise a full seven stories. Note the sharp triangular profile of these pilasters, the nuanced chromatic variations of the brickwork, and the rich terra cotta detailing on the upper levels.

The **Strand Bookshop** ㉙ at the corner of Broadway and 12th Street is the lone survivor in a neighborhood that was once the home of many publishers and booksellers. As you move north, have a look at the unusually handsome twin cast-iron facades at **827–831 Broadway** ㉚ (1866). Across the street don't miss Stephen D. Hatch's bright-red neo-Grec loft building at **836 Broadway** ㉛ (1876).

❷ Roosevelt Building

839–841 Broadway

1893 · STEPHEN D. HATCH

Teddy Roosevelt's grandfather's house stood on this block, and the family owned much of the land nearby. The Roosevelts built this imposing structure when the character of the neighborhood changed from residential to commercial.

Stephen Hatch's style evolved in the seventeen years after he designed 836 Broadway. Here he uses a blend of stone, Roman brick, and terra-cotta to create a solid Romanesque composition topped at the corner with a distinctive copper finial. The terra-cotta detailing is particularly appealing. Note that the twin shields flanking the Broadway entrance bear the letters R and B (Roosevelt Building).

West 29th

East 29th

West 28th

East 28th

5th Avenue

West 27th

East 27th

East 26th

Broadway

East 25th

East 24th

East 23rd

East 22nd

11

10

East 21st

8

East 20th

9   7

6

East 19th

4   5

3

2

East 18th

East 17th

C

Union Square West

Union Square East

Park Avenue South

D

E

East 16th

5th Avenue

1

A

East 15th

H

F

West 14th

G

Irving Place

East 13th

University Place

Broadway

4th Avenue

East 12th

1 Union Square

A Union Square Savings Bank

B Tammany Hall

C Century Building

D Decker Building

E Bank of the Metropolis

F Spingler Building

G Lincoln Building

H Tiffany & Company

2 MacIntyre Building

3 Hoyt Building

4 Arnold Constable Store

5 W & J Sloane Store (ABC Carpet)

6 Gorham Silver Manufacturing Company Building

7 Goelet Building

8 Warren Building

9 Lord & Taylor Dry Goods Store

10 929–933 Broadway

11 Mortimer Building

Union Square to 23rd Street

At 14th Street, Broadway seems to come to an abrupt halt at Union Square. On the map, it's easy to trace a diagonal through the square to 17th Street, where Broadway reasserts itself as a street. That route does not exist in reality, but the paths running north through the park reach the same destination with a jog to the west at 16th Street.

❶ Union Square

1839

Early New York's two main north–south arteries, Broadway (then known as Bloomingdale Road) and The Bowery, merge at 16th Street. This intersection was identified on the Commissioner's Plan of 1811 as Union Place. In 1839 Union Place was expanded to become a city park and was renamed Union Square in a successful attempt to spur residential development. With the opening of the Academy of Music on 14th Street in the mid-1850s, the area became the center of New York's "Rialto" theater district. Following the Civil War, the square was redesigned by Frederick Law Olmsted and Calvert Vaux, and the focus of the surrounding neighborhood shifted to retail. The history of Union Square is depicted in a series of bronze plaques inset in a bluestone strip in the sidewalk surrounding the park. The work of sculptor Gregg LeFevre, the scenes begin at 15th Street on the east side and follow the curve around 14th Street to 15th Street on the west.

Within the park a diverse collection of monuments is installed along the central axis. Facing out to 14th Street is a heroic equestrian image of George Washington (1856, Henry Kirke Brown and J. Q. A. Ward, with a pedestal by Richard Upjohn). Washington is shown on Evacuation Day, November 25, 1783, at the end of the Revolution when the British finally left New York. This is the first equestrian monument erected in the city since the gilded statue in Bowling Green of a mounted George III was pulled down by the Sons of Liberty in July 1776. The statues of the English King and the first American President were consciously based on the same famous statue of the Roman emperor Marcus Aurelius.

At the center of the park is the Independence Flagpole, with reliefs by Anthony de Francisi. Erected in 1926, the flagpole commemorates the 150th anniversary of the signing of the Declaration of Independence. It includes emblems for each of the thirteen original colonies, the text of the Declaration, and a frieze of life-size figures illustrating "the forces of oppression" and "the blessings of freedom and the enjoyment of happiness." Ironically, this civic-minded monument to the virtues of good government was commissioned by the members of the Tammany Society. At the north end of the park is a standing figure of Abraham Lincoln, also by Henry Kirke Brown. Monuments along the perimeter include a figure of Mohandis Gandhi (1986, Kantilal B. Patel) installed in its own garden, the James Fountain (1881, Karl Adolph Donndorf) on the west side, and the Marquis de Lafayette (1876, Frédéric-Auguste Bartholdi) on the east.

A handsome Beaux-Arts-style Park Pavilion (1929) marks the north end of the square. A graceful arch is flanked by a pair of loggias and crowned with a fine red-tile roof. The pavilion is a seasonal restaurant and overlooks the paved area that since 1976 has been the home of the celebrated Union Square Greenmarket.

⇢ Notable Buildings Around Union Square

Ⓐ Union Square Savings Bank

20 Union Square East
1905-7 · HENRY BACON

This serious, well-proportioned, and understated treasure box was designed by the architect of the Lincoln Memorial in Washington, D.C. A handsome Corinthian portico faces Union Square, taking full advantage of the prominent site. The bank is now a theater.

Ⓑ Tammany Hall

44 Union Square East
1928 · THOMPSON, HOLMES & CONVERSE WITH CHARLES BRADFORD MEYERS

The Tammany Society, New York's Democratic political machine, virtually controlled the city during the late nineteenth and early twentieth centuries. At the peak of its power in the 1920s the society erected this clubhouse as its headquarters. The Union Square facade of the building including the first-floor balcony under the portico was deliberately modelled on that of New York's original Federal Hall on Wall Street (demolished 1812) where Washington was inaugurated as our nation's first President.

By the early 1930s the extent of the society's graft and corruption was widely recognized, and Tammany Mayor James J. Walker was forced to resign in 1932. A decade later the society sold its meeting hall to the International Ladies Garment Workers' Union, and it became a major center for union activity. In 1984 the Roundabout Theater Company took over for a decade before heading uptown. The building is now being converted to office and retail use, but the exterior, including the Liberty Cap on the pediment facing Union Square, long a symbol of the society, has been preserved.

C Century Building

33 East 17th Street

1880–81 · WILLIAM SCHICKEL

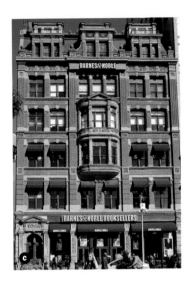

Warm red brick, crisp bluestone trim, and a two-story oriel window give this Queen Anne style commercial building a welcoming domestic aspect. Richly detailed terra-cotta panels and crisply carved stone surround the ground floor entrance, embellish the facade, and reappear in the treatment of the top floor dormers.

The Century Building was commissioned as a speculative undertaking by the Arnold and Constable families. In addition to their department store, they were among the largest landholders in late nineteenth-century New York. For much of the Century Building's life, it was the home of the celebrated *Century Magazine.*

D Decker Building

33 Union Square West

1892–93 · JOHN EDELMANN AND ALFRED ZUCKER

A little bit of Venice, echoes of the Alhambra and Louis Comfort Tiffany, and a large dose of the Chicago School are all brought together here with great panache. Early in his career Edelmann lived in Chicago where he was a mentor to the young Louis Sullivan. It's easy to spot their shared preference for a highly distinctive and complex style of shallow carved ornament. Here it enriches nearly every flat surface. The designers' underlying inspiration was always rooted in the natural world.

Plant forms are abstracted and stylized under the influence of Moorish decoration to create this lush patterning. The central tower is an Islamic extravaganza and was once topped by a minaret.

From 1967 to 1973 the sixth floor of the Decker Building housed Andy Warhol's celebrated Factory. It was here in 1968 that the artist was shot by Valerie Solanas. Warhol subsequently relocated the Factory diagonally across the street to 860 Broadway.

❺ Bank of the Metropolis

31 Union Square West
1903 · BRUCE PRICE

The familiar, sober classical vocabulary of bank architecture is enlivened here by a welcoming two-story bowed portico supported by a pair of gray granite Ionic columns facing Union Square. The long 16th Street elevation also features some distinctive touches. Notice the flattened arches floating in the openings of the ground level arcade and the lush foliate ornament in the panels under the windows higher up. A powerfully detailed balcony at the thirteenth story prepares the way for a bold copper cornice.

The block between 14th and 15th Streets offers two solid and accomplished historic structures: the **Spingler Building** ❻ (5 Union Square West, 1897, W. H. Hume and Sons) and the **Lincoln Building** ❼ (1 Union Square West, 1889, R. H. Robertson). The two facades share many compositional details, but one architect has chosen a classical vocabulary while the other has embraced the Romanesque.

More unusual is the contemporary building at 15 Union Square West. Behind the steel and glass are the arches of the cast iron facade from John Kellum's 1869 headquarters for **Tiffany & Company** ❽. The top seven floors were added to the original five when the building was converted to condominiums in 2009.

Between 17th and 18th Streets, the west side of Broadway retains three modest brick townhouses, the last of hundreds of such dwellings that were built in the 1840s when this was a residential area. At 18th Street, the character of the architecture shifts to reflect the surge of retail commerce that overtook the area in the late nineteenth century.

The Ladies Mile shopping district began downtown with the opening of the A. T. Stewart store on Broadway and Tenth Street in 1862. Over the next twenty years, high-end retailers erected substantial buildings along the entire stretch of Broadway between Union and Madison Squares. By the early 1880s enterprising shoppers could make a day of it, moving up Broadway from Stewart's store to 23rd Street. There they might rest and take refreshments at the Fifth Avenue Hotel before heading south again on Sixth Avenue.

Shopping continued into the evening, since the stretch of Broadway from 14th to 34th Street was the first to be illuminated with electricity. Arc lights were installed in 1880. Softer incandescent lighting followed not long after, and in 1892 the first illuminated billboard was in place, facing Madison Square.

As you walk north from 17th Street, you will notice that sections of Broadway's roadway have been cordoned off for pedestrian use. These efforts, which extend north to Columbus Circle, are part of the Broadway Boulevard project begun by Mayor Michael Bloomberg in 2008. They have transformed street life. Traffic has been dramatically reduced, and in its place there are welcoming chairs, tables, umbrellas, colorful planters, CitiBike racks, and more often than not, a variety of pop-up food and refreshment stands.

❷ MacIntyre Building

874 Broadway

1890–92 · R. H. ROBERTSON

Named for its builder, a successful pharmacist, the MacIntyre Building occupies a prominent corner site and is a handsome anchor for this stretch of Broadway. The elevation is complex, unfolding upward through a succession of materials and styles. The composition

culminates in the corner tower which features a wealth of fanciful decoration based on an eclectic mix of historical precedents.

❸ Hoyt Building

873 Broadway

1868, 1888 · GRIFFITH THOMAS

Commissioned by merchant Edwin Hoyt, this building was home to a series of dry-goods stores as well as the offices of Herter Brothers, the celebrated interior decorating firm. Today the ground floor detailing has been compromised, but the upper floors remain much as designed. The elevation is a Renaissance composition executed in marble and contained at either end by strongly cut quoins. The central part of the 18th Street facade is simpler and flatter. The more assertive western section is an addition from the 1880s, as is the top story of the Broadway facade.

❹ Arnold Constable Store

881–887 Broadway

1868–77 · GRIFFITH THOMAS

Griffith Thomas received the commissions for the Hoyt and the Arnold Constable buildings at the same time, and he clearly worked hard to ensure that the two were visually compatible. In 1872, however,

Thomas was asked to expand the Arnold Constable building. He responded by adding a fashionable Second Empire mansard roof. Further additions eventually extended the store the full length of the 19th Street block, all the way to Fifth Avenue.

Once again, the side-street facade is much simpler and less plastic in its detailing. And while the Broadway facade is marble, the matching Fifth Avenue facade was executed in less expensive cast iron. Arnold Constable was the second largest store in New York at the time of its relocation from Canal Street to Broadway. In 1914 the firm relocated again to Fifth Avenue and 40th Street. When it closed in 1975, it was the oldest department store in the city.

❺ W & J Sloane Store

(ABC Carpet)

888 Broadway

1881–82 · W. WHEELER SMITH

The financial panic of 1873 had an enormous impact on the retail business in New York. No new stores were built along Broadway

until the early 1880s. By this time stylistic preferences had shifted as demonstrated by the W & J Sloane store. Instead of flamboyant mansard roofs and gleaming marble, the store, built for New York's premier merchants of rugs and carpets, is sober and understated.

But the building repays longer examination. Notice the careful, rhythmic composition of the facade and the thoughtful way the architect has grouped the floors together. The structure of the building is clear and logical. At the same time, the understated, almost hidden entrance is both mysterious and inviting.

Although there is little here that is overtly fancy, this is still a luxury building. Smith has carefully orchestrated the materials—stone, brick, iron, and terra-cotta—to create a rich, warm palette. Notice the restrained classical motifs on the pilasters and the decorative terra-cotta panels. The narrative details (birds, swags, cupids, rich foliage) are charming, and the fabrication is of high quality.

❻ Gorham Silver Manufacturing Company Building

889–891 Broadway
1883–84 · EDWARD H. KENDALL

Here is the deliberately quaint and picturesque Queen Anne style in its full expression. The building was originally designed for two purposes. It housed the headquarters of the silver company with a series of apartments on the upper floors, which may account for its somewhat domestic personality.

Today the steeply pitched roof, the stepped gables inspired by traditional Dutch and Flemish practice, and the decorative terra-cotta work all survive in good part. Much of the fanciful original detailing has disappeared, including the minaret that once topped the corner gable, but the rich terra-cotta panels and the wrought-iron sunflowers on the 19th Street facade are intact.

Nearly all the land on both sides of Broadway between 19th and 20th Street was owned by the Goelet family. Their patronage produced a group of very handsome buildings in the block ahead.

❼ Goelet Building

900 Broadway

1886–87 · STANFORD WHITE OF MCKIM, MEAD & WHITE; ENLARGED 1906, MAYNICKE & FRANKE

Stanford White's original building was five stories tall and culminated in an elegant Roman cornice above a handsome attic. In 1906 the cornice and attic were removed, and four additional stories added. In the process, much of the building's balance and classical coherence were lost. Today it's best to concentrate on the lower floors where White's elegant sensibility can still be appreciated. The proportions are subtle, the detailing fine, and the balance of brick, stone, and terra-cotta perfectly calibrated. The soft chromatic modulations and understated surface textures are beautifully done. Look at the suave, assured way the arcade turns the corner from Broadway to 20th Street. The tall stilted arches supported by polished granite columns add extra drama to the corner.

❽ Warren Building

907 Broadway

1890 · STANFORD WHITE OF
MCKIM, MEAD & WHITE

Although the underlying
elevations and proportions of
the Warren and Goelet buildings
are essentially the same, the
two structures could not be less
alike in their social personality.
Where the Goelet Building is
sleek and self-contained, the
Warren Building is bejeweled and
extroverted. The quality of the carving is stunning, and the architect
has a beautiful way of playing decorative terra-cotta trim against thin,
pale, Roman brick. What a pleasure to have two such different works by
the same remarkable architect opposite one another.

❾ Lord & Taylor Dry Goods Store

901 Broadway

1869–70 · JAMES H. GILES

Like many other department stores, Lord & Taylor began downtown and moved north as the shopping district marched up Broadway. This building was the firm's third. When it was completed in 1870, the Lord & Taylor store was the epitome of contemporary architectural fashion. James H. Giles pulled out all the stops, taking full advantage of advances in iron-casting technology. Originally, the store stretched along most of the west side of Broadway between 19th and 20th Streets. Most of this is gone now, but the centerpiece of the design, the striking diagonal corner tower, remains. Just about every motif in the vocabulary of architectural ornament appears somewhere in this richly sculptural extravaganza.

Lord & Taylor was a pioneer in marketing ready-made clothing. Isaac Singer's invention of the sewing machine in the 1850s made possible the mass production of uniforms during the Civil War. When the conflict ended, Lord & Taylor adapted the process to civilian clothing. Before they offered "off the rack" garments, department stores sold materials—fabrics, buttons, trim, and other notions. A tailor, dressmaker, or skilled homemaker would then fashion a garment from these "dry goods." Lord & Taylor was also a pioneer in devising the elaborate Christmas window displays that are so much a part of the holidays in New York.

As you walk north, don't miss the three small houses at **929, 931, and 933 Broadway ❿**, all built around 1846. They have been much altered, but still provide a sense of what this stretch of Broadway was like in the mid-nineteenth century.

⓫ Mortimer Building

935 Broadway

1861–62 · GRIFFITH THOMAS

The Mortimer Building was among the first commercial structures erected along this section of Broadway. Designed at the start of the architect's career, for a family that would go on to control large parcels of Manhattan real estate, the building is an elegantly understated Italian palazzo in light brownstone rising over a classically detailed ground floor in cast iron. The Mortimer Building still has a quiet presence and dignity that is very appealing in spite of the fact that in 1912 the roof was raised and an attic floor inserted.

East 34th

West 33rd

East 33rd

West 32nd

West 32nd

East 32nd

West 31st

East 31st

15

West 30th

East 30th

West 29th

East 29th

13

14
12   10
11

West 28th

East 28th

9   8

East 27th

7

G

East 26th

5   6

F

4

A

East 25th

E

East 24th

D

3

West 23rd

2   1

B

East 22nd

East 21st

East 20th

East 19th

1 Flatiron Building

2 West Union Telegraph Building

3 Fifth Avenue Building clock

A Admiral David Glasgow Farragut

B One Madison Park

C 45 East 22nd Street

D Metropolitan Life Tower

E Metropolitan Life North Building

F Appellate Division, New York
State Supreme Court

G New York Life Insurance
Company Building

4 Townsend Building

5 St. James Building

6 1132 Broadway

7 1149 Broadway

8 Johnston Building

9 Baudouine Building

10 Centurion Building

11 1180 Broadway

12 1201 Broadway

13 Gilsey House

14 Hotel Breslin

15 Grand Hotel

6th Avenue

5th Avenue

Broadway

Broadway

23rd Street to 32nd Street

❶ Flatiron Building

(originally Fuller Building)

945 Broadway

1901–3 · D. H. BURNHAM & COMPANY

The Flatiron Building has often been likened to a great ocean liner sailing up Fifth Avenue. That description is an apt one. This is a building of extraordinary drama, romance, and dynamism with a remarkable taut, compressed energy.

The building sits on a tight triangular site. On the east and west sides, sheer walls rise straight to the cornice from the lot line. The wall planes converge at a curved northern apex that is only six feet wide. (The small steel-and-glass pavilion at street level at the northern tip was added against the architect's wishes to provide additional rentable space. Burnham would have preferred that his building rise unimpeded on all sides.) The building's height (23 stories) and its eye-catching thinness make the structure visually powerful but also create a certain amount of anxiety. Early observers truly worried that it might blow over.

In addition to the sculptural drama of its form, this is a building of great ornamental richness and subtlety. Decorative terra-cotta panels cover every square inch, and the carefully calibrated repertoire of loosely French Renaissance motifs brings the flat wall surfaces to life. Three slightly protruding bays to break up what might otherwise be static slabs of masonry.

The Flatiron was erected by the George A. Fuller Company, a leading Chicago construction firm, as its New York headquarters. The first tall building north of 14th Street, it was designed to attract attention. Two years later, in 1904, Cyrus Eidlitz would emulate the Flatiron in his design for the New York Times Building on 42nd Street.

Just to the west of the Flatiron Building at the corner of Fifth Avenue and 23rd Street is Henry Hardenbergh's **West Union Telegraph Building ❷** (1884), a picturesque composition in red brick, limestone, and terra-cotta.

Across 23rd Street on the west side of the pedestrian plaza is the block-long **Fifth Avenue Building** with its gold **sidewalk clock ❸,** installed in 1909 to coincide with the building's completion. This was once the site of the old Fifth Avenue Hotel.

⬦ Madison Square Park

The Commissioner's Plan of 1811 reserved a plot of land between 23rd and 34th Streets from Third to Seventh Avenue as a "Parade" or military drill field. Commercial development soon encroached on this space, and in 1847 the city created what is now Madison Square Park.

Over the years the personality of Madison Square and its surroundings evolved along much the same lines as Union Square. By the 1860s the area had become a fashionable residential quarter. Later in the century, spurred by the opening of Madison Square Garden at 26th Street, the park became the center of a thriving entertainment, restaurant, and hotel district. By the early 1890s, Broadway north of 23rd Street emerged as the first "Great White Way" thanks to the introduction of the city's first electric signage. By the turn of the twentieth century, the entertainment center had moved north toward what is now Times Square, and Madison Square evolved into a business center.

Since the 1870s when Madison Square Park was redesigned by William Grant and Ignatz Pilatz, who had worked with Olmsted and Vaux on Central Park, this has been a welcoming site for public sculpture. The torch from the Statue of Liberty was on view here from the centennial year of 1876 to 1884 as part of an effort to raise funds for the construction of the statue's pedestal. Today the park's sculptures celebrate Republican politicians: Chester Alan Arthur (George Edwin Bissell, 1898), the twenty-first President; William H. Seward (Randolph Rogers, 1876), Secretary of State for Presidents Lincoln and Johnson; and Senator Roscoe Conkling (J.Q. A. Ward, 1893). More significant is the monument to naval hero **Admiral David Glasgow Farragut** 🅐 by Augustus Saint-Gaudens on a base by Stanford White (1881). Unlike traditional static figures on high pedestals, Farragut is stalwart and filled with energy, standing on an exedra intended to invite viewers to approach. The reliefs in the base, Courage and Loyalty, are almost art nouveau in their delicacy; an unwavering upright sword at the center floats above the abstracted waves in the background.

The **Eternal Light Flagstaff** on the west side of the park

(Thomas Hastings and Paul Wayland Bartlett, 1924) honors those who served in World War I.

The park is managed by the Madison Square Park Conservancy, a public/private partnership that maintains the landscape and presents lively programming. Since 2004 the Conservancy has commissioned a remarkable series of public art installations in the square.

ⓑ One Madison Park

23 East 22rd Street
2009 · CETRA RUDDY

While much of the Gramercy, Flatiron, Union Square, and Ladies Mile neighborhoods are incorporated in historic districts that restrict development, this site lies just outside those boundaries. This elegant glass 60-story tower extends through the block to 22nd Street. Multistory blocks of apartments cantilever to the east from a dark gray service core, the verticality broken every several stories by an indentation. Visible to the east from Madison Square is the faceted form of **45 East 22nd Street ⓒ**, another beneficiary of the gap in historic district protection.

ⓓ Metropolitan Life Tower
(New York Edition Hotel)

1 Madison Avenue
1907 · PIERRE LE BRUN OF NAPOLEON LE BRUN AND SONS; 1960, MORGAN AND MERONI

In 1902, just as Metropolitan Life was preparing plans for a major new headquarters building, the celebrated bell tower in Venice's St. Mark's Square collapsed. This beloved monument was subsequently rebuilt, thanks in large part to the support of J.P. Morgan. The event clearly affected Pierre LeBrun. His design for Met Life's tower expands the Venetian campanile to fifty stories and adds a prominent clock face two-thirds of the way up on each side.

LeBrun's original design was a richly monumental, organic one. Today only its basic outline survives. Between 1960 and 1964 the firm of Morgan and Meroni undertook a comprehensive redesign of the entire Met Life complex. In the process a good deal of LeBrun's original decoration was removed. The tower still dominates its corner of the park and has kept its key features: the crowning loggia, the pyramidal cupola, and the twenty-seven-foot clocks.

❺ Metropolitan Life North Building

11–25 Madison Avenue
1932 · HARVEY WILEY CORBETT AND D. EVERETT WAID

During the 1920s, the expanding insurance firm commissioned Harvey Corbett to design a new building one block north of their existing home. Corbett and his patrons were ambitious. The building was to be an art deco colossus, rising 100 stories and filling the entire block between Madison Avenue and Park Avenue South from 24th to 25th Street. With the stock market crash, the project was dramatically scaled back. What exists today is essentially the 25-story base of the proposed tower.

❻ Appellate Division, New York State Supreme Court

35 East 25th Street
1896–99 · JAMES BROWN LORD

The Appellate Court House embodies the principles of classical architecture in the service of democracy presented at the Chicago World's Columbian Exposition of 1893. Lord embraced its premise that architecture, sculpture, painting, and the decorative arts could be marshalled to work together to create buildings that would impress, inspire, and educate a nation's citizens.

A handsome marble screen of colossal Corinthian columns faces Madison Square. The entablature supports four caryatids by Thomas Shields Clarke representing the Four Seasons. At the roofline is Karl Bitter's personification of Peace. On the 25th Street side, figures of Wisdom and Strength by Frederick Ruskstull flank the stairs leading up to a screen of six columns supporting a heavily decorated entablature.

In the pediment Charles Henry Niehaus's group depicts the *Triumph of Law*. The presiding figures at the apex are Daniel Chester French's *Justice,* flanked by *Power* and *Study.* Finally, arrayed around the building at the roofline are historical lawgivers: Confucius, Moses, Zoroaster, Alfred the Great, Lycurgus, Solon, and others. Mohammed was removed in 1955 at the request of the Islamic community.

The public spaces inside the Appellate Court House are magnificent. The overall decorative program, coordinated by John La Farge, features an ambitious cycle of allegorical murals related to the law. A full roster of America's best turn-of-the-century painters is represented, including Willard Metcalf, H. Siddons Mowbray, and Edwin Blashfield. Custom furniture was provided by Herter Brothers.

❼ New York Life Insurance Company Building

51 Madison Avenue
1928 · CASS GILBERT

This is the third of Gilbert's major skyscrapers, built a little more than a decade after the Woolworth Building. Although there is still restrained historic ornament here and there, this is a far simpler structure. The design is a big step toward the stripped-down art deco towers of the 1930s, such as the Empire State Building at Fifth Avenue and 34th Street. Apparently, Gilbert lost effective control of his design during construction. This may explain the building's somewhat blocky appearance and the slightly awkward arrangement of the setbacks. The New York Life Building occupies a distinguished site: Stanford White's Madison Square Garden stood here from 1890 to 1925.

At 24th Street, Broadway and Fifth Avenue intersect at Worth Square. The obelisk (James Goodwin Batterson, 1857) at the northern end of the triangle honors General William Jenkins Worth, a hero of the War of 1812, the Seminole Wars, and the Mexican American War.

The next section of Broadway, stretching north from 25th to 33rd Streets, prospered first as an entertainment district with hotels, clubs, stores, and apartments before becoming a mercantile district of offices and lofts. Now known as NoMad, the neighborhood is very much in transition. Wholesalers of jewelry, watches, and wigs are interspersed with fashionable restaurants and trendy hotels. In addition to the renovation of existing buildings, two very large modern hotels are also rising. The Virgin Hotel (VOA Architects) will soon open at 1225 Broadway, and construction is underway for a Ritz Carlton Hotel designed by Rafael Vinoly at 1185 Broadway.

At 25th Street is Cyrus Eidlitz's dignified **Townsend Building** ❹ of 1896 (1121 Broadway). Bruce Price's **St. James Building** ❺ (1896–98) at 1133 Broadway features an arched entry with a stylish oculus above and elaborate ornament below a projecting cornice. Across the street at **1132 Broadway** ❻ (1901), John B. Snook's tall, thin, and richly plastic composition was originally built as bachelor apartments. In the next block, the Romanesque Revival **1149 Broadway** ❼ (DeLemos & Cordes, 1886) offers simple rustic detailing and bold carved lettering that identify the original owners: Wallace & Co.

Twenty-Eighth Street brings us to the home of the original Tin Pan Alley—the epicenter of the American popular music business in the late-nineteenth and early-twentieth centuries. The blocks of 28th Street on either side of Broadway were a mecca for composers and music publishers. There's a well-worn plaque set in the sidewalk just east of Broadway on the south side of the street.

❽ Johnston Building

(NoMad Hotel)

1170 Broadway
1903 · SCHICKEL & DITMARS

This turn-of-the-century building manages to blend restraint and exuberance in just the right proportions. The rounded corner pavilion topped by a lantern is a motif repeated in the blocks to come. It's an effective way to allow a building with frontages on both the side street and avenue to turn the corner with grace and style.

❾ Baudouine Building

1181 Broadway
1896 · ALFRED ZUCKER

A four-story rusticated base, an intermediate cornice on the 28th Street facade bearing the builder's name, and a richly detailed classical pediment facing north only partially prepare us for the miniature Greek temple perched at the top.

Ancient Greece makes another appearance on the facade of the **Centurion Building** ❿ of 1910 at 1182 Broadway. Here architect William Rouse has concentrated his classicism at street level with a strongly detailed row of four fluted Doric columns supporting a projecting entablature.

Next door at **1180 Broadway** ⓫, Stephen D. Hatch's cast-iron facade of 1870 is a reminder of an earlier and more modest era. Across the street there is some fine Art Deco detailing on the frieze at **1201 Broadway** ⓬.

⓭ Gilsey House

1200 Broadway

1869–71 · STEPHEN D. HATCH AND DANIEL D. BADGER

This Second Empire extravaganza was built when this stretch of Broadway was at the center of the city's entertainment district. Gilsey House and the Grand Hotel two blocks north are the only survivors from a group of fashionable hotels that strove to outdo each other in continental opulence. Gilsey House borrows its stylish vocabulary of mansard roofs, dormers, colonnades, elaborate corner pavilions, and bold plasticity from the celebrated New Louvre (1852–57) in Paris. The building is impressive even in its current simplified and stripped-down form. Notice how the facade along 29th Street is stepped back to avoid overwhelming the narrow side street. The fake clock face at the top of the corner pavilion is an unfortunate addition.

Mark Twain, Oscar Wilde, and Diamond Jim Brady were all patrons of this landmark of a bygone era in the Tenderloin district.

⓮ Hotel Breslin
(Ace Hotel)

1186 Broadway
1903–4 · CLINTON & RUSSELL

Built thirty years after the theatrical Gilsey House, the Breslin's turn-of-the-century restraint has much more in common with the Johnson Building to the south than its immediate neighbor. At the Breslin the balance between the areas of variegated brick and limestone is carefully calibrated. The larger windows on each facade are linked vertically by stone trim and separated by terra-cotta panels,

drawing the eye upward. Between these vertical stacks broad areas of brick are pierced by smaller openings. Notice how the architects rather than carrying their rounded corner tower all the way down to street level have set it back and above the building's sturdy rectangular stone base with its handsome iron and glass windows.

⑮ Grand Hotel

1232–38 Broadway

1868 · HENRY ENGELBERT

Here is an alternative version of the French Second Empire architectural style. Compared with the Gilsey House, the Grand Hotel is
more disciplined and restrained. Although the lower floors, originally
cast iron, have been completely remodeled, the upper stories
are remarkably intact. The richly modelled facade is executed in
white marble with projecting pavilions, highlighted by strong quoins.
The window surrounds on each floor, separated by strong horizontal
cornices, are slightly different. A deep surmounting cornice
with vigorous brackets introduces the dark mansard roof and
exuberant dormers.

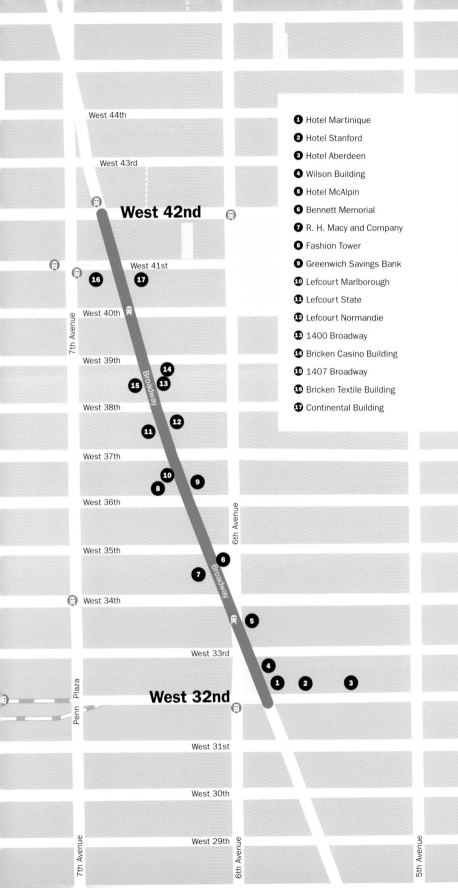

West 44th

West 43rd

West 42nd

West 41st

West 40th

West 39th

West 38th

West 37th

West 36th

West 35th

West 34th

West 33rd

West 32nd

West 31st

West 30th

West 29th

7th Avenue

Broadway

6th Avenue

5th Avenue

Penn Plaza

❶ Hotel Martinique
❷ Hotel Stanford
❸ Hotel Aberdeen
❹ Wilson Building
❺ Hotel McAlpin
❻ Bennett Memorial
❼ R. H. Macy and Company
❽ Fashion Tower
❾ Greenwich Savings Bank
❿ Lefcourt Marlborough
⓫ Lefcourt State
⓬ Lefcourt Normandie
⓭ 1400 Broadway
⓮ Bricken Casino Building
⓯ 1407 Broadway
⓰ Bricken Textile Building
⓱ Continental Building

32nd Street to 42nd Street

Up to this point, whenever Broadway's diagonal path has crossed a major north–south avenue, the result has been a handsome park (Union Square and Madison Square). As we move north, these intersections become less verdant. Thirty-Second Street is the base of the first of what may be called squares but are in fact triangular traffic islands. Each intersection has two of them, one to the north, one to the south. Together they form an hourglass shape.

The intersection of Broadway and Sixth Avenue creates two such distinct "squares." Both derive their names from the neighborhood's close association with the newspaper industry at the turn of the twentieth century: Greeley Square, between 32nd and 33rd Streets, and Herald Square, between 34th and 35th Streets, south of the former site of the New York Herald Building.

At the south end of Greeley Square is a seated figure of the politician and founder of the *New York Tribune,* Horace Greeley. The Hotel Martinique faces the square on the east.

❶ Hotel Martinique

1260–66 Broadway

1897–1911 · HENRY J. HARDENBERGH

Based on the success of his design for the original Waldorf-Astoria Hotel on what is now the site of the Empire State Building, Hardenbergh was a logical choice when property owner William R. H. Martin wanted to build a luxury hotel on fast-developing Greeley Square. Coyly named for the owner, the Martinique is clad in terra-cotta and limestone.

It features a bold mansard roof and rich French Renaissance detailing. Applied shell decoration enlivens the wall surfaces of the top three stories. The hotel originally included a restaurant with décor modelled on the Apollo Room at the Louvre.

Next door to the Martinique is the **Hotel Stanford ❷** (1905), with a handsome Italianate facade. The row of balconies at the fourth level is beautifully detailed. Farther along at 17 West 32nd Street, the **Aberdeen ❸** (1890s) has one of the most exuberant Beaux-Arts entry portals of any New York building. Note the bare-chested Atalantes supporting the improbably truncated columns, the swelling pediment, and the thickly encrusted giant consoles.

❹ Wilson Building

1270 Broadway
1911–12 · ROUSE & GOLDSTONE

This office building is a good neighbor to the Martinique. It retains its original cast-iron shop fronts and features a particularly handsome crown with a crisply detailed projecting cornice.

❺ Hotel McAlpin
(Herald Towers)

1300 Broadway (50 West 34th Street)
1911–12 · FRANK MILLS ANDREWS

When it opened, the McAlpin was the largest hotel in the world.

Innovations included a separate floor for women traveling alone, a quiet floor for night workers who needed to sleep during the day, an in-house hospital, ship-to-shore radio links, and a top-floor Turkish bath and pool. In the basement, the Marine Grill was decorated with a remarkable set of twenty terra-

cotta panels depicting scenes of the New York Harbor. Removed in the 1970s, the panels are now installed, along with the restaurant's handsome iron entry gate, in the Fulton Center subway station on lower Broadway. Today the hotel's 1,500 rooms have been reconfigured into condominium apartments.

Above modern dark marble shopfronts, the twenty-five-story building rises over a sturdy rusticated stone base and culminates in an elaborate crown with distinctive terra-cotta detailing. On the Broadway side, the architect inserted deep light wells to bring illumination to the interior bedrooms. At the fourth floor, where these light wells meet the building's base, the compressed space is bridged by a pair of Tuscan columns supporting a lintel and cartouche.

❻ Bennett Memorial

Herald Square

1939 ·AYMAR EMBURY II

This memorial to newspaper publishers James Gordon Bennett and his son, James Gordon Bennett Jr., incorporates decorative elements from the facade of the New York Herald Building, whose main entrance was directly across 35th Street. In 1890 the younger Bennett commissioned McKim, Mead

& White to build a new home for his successful daily newspaper. The south facade of the building featured two large clocks and a bronze sculptural group including the goddess Minerva and two stalwart hammer-wielding bell ringers by sculptor Antonin Jean Paul Carles. A flock of twenty-two bronze owls was arrayed along the cornice.

The Herald Building has been demolished, but the clocks and sculptural group live on as part of the memorial. Come by on the hour to hear the bell rung or at night to study the two remaining bronze owls. Their eyes light up with an eerie green glow.

Although there is little direct evidence at street level, Herald Square is an underground transportation crossroads. Beneath the surface is a dense network of rail lines. Long Island Railroad and Amtrak trains pass underneath on their way from Penn Station to the East River tunnels. The PATH line from Hoboken and Jersey City terminates at 33rd Street and Broadway. It's also a subway hub including the N, Q, R, and W on the BMT line as well as the B, D, F, and M on the IND Sixth Avenue line.

As always, real estate development arrived with mass transportation. Ease of access was a key reason why Herald Square quickly developed into a major shopping center. The dominant retail presence today is, of course, Macy's.

❼ R. H. Macy and Company

Broadway and 34th Street
1901–2 · DELEMOS & CORDES
1924, 1928, 1931 ADDITIONS BY
ROBERT D. KOHN

In 1902 Macy's moved from 14th Street to this nine-story building. It was designed to be both eye-catching and dignified. Constructed of brick and limestone and carefully detailed, the building set a new standard for large department stores. The main entrance on 34th Street is adorned with a handsome clock and graceful caryatid figures by R. Massey Rhind.

New wings were added in 1924, 1928, and finally in 1931, by which time the store occupied nearly the entire block from Broadway to

Seventh Avenue and from 34th to 35th Street. At more than one million square feet, Macy's was proud to proclaim itself the largest store in the world. Note how as you move westward from the original Broadway building, the style of each addition changes to follow contemporary architectural fashion. By the time you reach Seventh Avenue, classicism has given way to art deco.

While Macy's appears to occupy a full city block, this is not strictly the case. At the corner of Broadway and 34th Street there is a small parcel of land, purchased at great cost by a rival with the specific intention of thwarting Macy's expansion. Isidore and Nathan Straus, who owned Macy's, were undeterred. They simply built their building around the corner parcel where an independently owned storefront business continues to operate.

Macy's presence soon inspired rivals to stake their claim in the neighborhood. In 1901 Saks and Company opened a large store at 1311 Broadway across 34th Street, and in 1908 the Gimbel Brothers followed suit with a D. H. Burnham building at 1275 Broadway. Not much remains today of either of these buildings. However, do not miss the urbane copper-clad art deco bridge (1925; Shreve, Lamb & Harmon) that connected the Gimbels store to its warehouse across 32nd Street.

North of Macy's is the garment district, long the center of clothing manufacturing in New York. Following the tragic 1911 Triangle Shirtwaist fire, the city enacted a series of new health and safety regulations designed to protect workers in loft buildings. These laws, combined with the effects of the city's new zoning regulations of 1916, forced much of the garment trade out of its traditional home on the Lower East Side. The establishment of the Herald Square retail district and the increased availability of rail transportation on Manhattan's West Side made the neighborhood attractive for manufacturing. The garment industry moved in, establishing itself in the upper 30s between Broadway and Seventh Avenue.

Garment district buildings, such as 1333 and 1350 Broadway, are generally understated and functional in design. A notable exception is Fashion Tower, an extravagant celebration of the industry.

❽ Fashion Tower

135–39 West 36th Street
1922–25 · EMERY ROTH

This is truly a monument to
the world of fashion. There
are polychromed terra-cotta
peacocks over the entries.
Flanking the building's name are winged putti holding shears and
drapery fabric. In the spandrels at the fifth floor, seated figures admire
themselves in handheld mirrors. The building, executed in rich, warm
sandstone with cast iron trim and window frames, shows the art
nouveau style morphing into art deco.

   Next door and across the street, 141 and 142 West 36th are also
worth looking at for their enthusiastic terra-cotta embellishment.

❾ Greenwich Savings Bank
(The Haier Building)

1352 Broadway
1922–24 · YORK & SAWYER

The Greenwich Savings Bank is a true temple of finance: solid,
dignified, and classic. On Broadway a monumental Corinthian
colonnade is set on a high podium and surmounted by a substantial
attic. Behind the colonnade three tall arched windows admit light into
a large elliptical banking hall. Spare and unadorned, the building owes
stylistic debts both to ancient Rome and to French classicism of the
eighteenth century.

   The three street facades use the same architectural vocabulary, but
to slightly different effect. On 36th Street the columns are engaged
rather than freestanding;
there are few windows and no
entries. The Sixth Avenue facade
mirrors the one on Broadway,
but because of the irregular
trapezoidal shape of the lot,
this elevation is narrower. The
entire design has been skillfully
compressed to fit the space.

A good number of the buildings in this neighborhood were erected by developers Abraham Lefcourt and Abraham Bricken, both of whom began their careers in the clothing business. The buildings they commissioned are handsome, unpretentious, and reso-

lutely commercial. The **Lefcourt Marlborough** ❿ at 1359 Broadway (1925, George & Edward Blum), the **Lefcourt State** ⓫ at 1375 (1928, Buchman & Kahn), and the **Lefcourt Normandie** ⓬ at 1384 (1928, Bark & Djorup) are by different architects, but are essentially the same building, differentiated by individualized classical detailing.

Some of the best buildings in the neighborhood were designed by Ely Jacques Kahn, one of New York's great art deco designers and an architect with a reputation for pragmatism and style. Two of Kahn's most appealing and elaborate Garment District buildings fill the block on the east side of Broadway between 38th and 39th Streets. **1400 Broadway** ⓭ offers appealing art deco terra-cotta panels, stylish red window frames, and a rhythmic series of setbacks at the upper stories. The **Bricken Casino Building** ⓮ (1410 Broadway), is named for the Casino Theater, which once occupied the site. Its design is more restrained. The black-and-white brickwork on the upper floors is beautifully balanced. Near street level, the polished black granite and dark bronze gleam. The setbacks up top are carefully coordinated with those of 1400 Broadway next door. Both buildings date from 1930.

⓯ 1407 Broadway

1948–50 · KAHN & JACOBS

This sleek brick-and-aluminum tower was once detailed in a distinctive palette of pinks and greens. (Sadly, the pink vertical panels separating the windows were removed in 2015. The canopied entrance and gleaming white lobby date to 2018.) By employing a podium-like base and setting his tower back from the street on all sides, Kahn's successor partner Robert Jacobs moves his design toward the sheer glass boxes of the postwar International Style. Acknowledging Broadway's diagonal path, the three-story podium is placed parallel to the street, but the tower above pivots to conform with the city's grid. At the corner of 39th Street both sections, base and tower, are allowed to merge. Seen from street level, the effect is dynamic and energized.

The design of 1407 Broadway stresses the horizontal. Across the street at 1411 Broadway, the architects have gone in the opposite direction. Their building is all about verticals. The contrast between the two facing buildings is striking.

15

⑯ Bricken Textile Building

1441 Broadway

1929 · ELY JACQUES KAHN

At the center of the facade, wedge-shaped yellow brick pilasters draw the eye upward. Flanking sections in dark brown brick are detailed with horizontal bands to provide balance. Panels of the same dark brick inserted under the windows of the central section tie this boldly textural art deco design together. Above the 17th floor, where the setbacks begin, contrasting blocks of yellow and brown brick are asymmetrically arranged to reflect the geometries of the building.

Across the way is another Kahn building, designed one year later in a very different style.

⑰ Continental Building

1450 Broadway

1930–31 · ELY JACQUES KAHN

This nearly ornament-free tower is executed in pale brick above a base of bright white limestone. A series of setbacks culminates in a tall, thin tower. Kahn has shifted the axis of this tower to conform not to the slanted course of Broadway but to the Manhattan street grid. This is the same design strategy we encountered at 1407 Broadway and at the Standard Oil Building downtown.

West 58th

West 57th

West 56th

West 55th

West 54th

West 53rd

West 52nd

West 51st

West 50th

West 49th

West 48th

West 47th

West 46th

West 45th

West 44th

West 43rd

West 42nd

West 41st

Broadway

7th Avenue

7th Avenue

1 Times Square
2 Knickerbocker Hotel
A Bush Tower
B Condé Nast Building
C Bank of America Tower
3 Paramount Theater Building
4 New York Times Annex
5 One Astor Plaza
6 Lyceum Theater
7 Marriott Marquis Hotel
8 I Miller Building
9 George M. Cohan Statue
10 Father Francis P. Duffy Statue
11 tkts Booth
12 Bleachers
13 Palace Theatre
14 Brill Building
15 Winter Garden Theater
16 Hollywood/Mark Hellinger Theater
17 Hammerstein's Theater
18 Ford Motor Company Building
19 Woodward Hotel
20 Hotel Carlton
21 Mutual Life Insurance Building
A Peerless Motor Car and A.T. Demarest Buildings
B Central Park Tower
C American Fine Arts Society
D American Society of Civil Engineers Building
E Hearst Magazine Building

Times Square to 57th Street

For many people, the blocks ahead evoke the word "Broadway": bright lights, surging crowds, vibrant energy. For more than a century, Times Square ➊ has been the center of New York's entertainment district. The story begins in 1904 when the IRT subway opened. Trains moved north from City Hall to Grand Central Terminal and then west across 42nd Street to Broadway. The arrival of efficient transportation to what was then known as Longacre Square was followed by an explosion of real estate development.

The same year the subway opened, Adolph Ochs, publisher of the *New York Times,* commissioned Cyrus L. W. Eidlitz to design a new headquarters on the wedge of land on 42nd Street where Broadway and Seventh Avenue converged. The 24-story Times Tower, then the tallest building north of City Hall, was an instant landmark, and Longacre Square was promptly rechristened Times Square by the city's Board of Aldermen. The tradition of marking the arrival of each New Year with the drop of an illuminated ball from the Times Tower began in 1907. Today Eidlitz's tower still stands but stripped of its original detailing and encrusted with signage, it is virtually unrecognizable.

1904 also saw the opening of the now-vanished Hotel Astor, which filled the entire block between 44th and 45th Streets on the west side of Broadway. The hotel, a project of William

Waldorf Astor, was an immediate and dramatic success. Its richly decorated ballrooms and roof garden quickly became fashionable gathering
places for a growing middle-class clientele and established Times
Square as a social and entertainment center.

Immediately opposite the Astor, on the east side of Broadway, stood
theatrical impresario Oscar Hammerstein's Olympia Theater complex.
Erected in 1895, the theater was among the first of dozens that
would soon occupy the side streets off Broadway. Ablaze with electric
signage, the Olympia, now demolished, was a herald of even brighter
lights to come.

By the end of the first decade of the twentieth century, Times Square
had become a vibrant, dynamic social and entertainment mecca. For
more than a half-century, the neighborhood was synonymous with all
that was glamorous and sophisticated about New York. By the 1970s,
however, Times Square had become dangerous and unsavory. Dirt,
crime, and pornography proliferated. The city's Economic Development
Corporation and New York State, working with private development
partners, stepped in. The 42nd Street Development Corporation, led by
architect Robert A.M. Stern and designer Tibor Kalman, recommended
that plans for revitalization should stress entertainment and tourism.
Exuberant architectural design and prominent electronic signage were
encouraged. The renewal process began with anti-pornography zoning
and increased police patrols. Tax incentives followed. Then in 1982
the city created a Special Midtown Zoning District where new buildings
were allowed to be 20 percent larger than otherwise permitted. The in-
tent was to encourage the development of offices, hotels, retail space,
and restaurants facing Times Square. The initiative was a success. In
2009 Broadway was closed to traffic from 42nd to 47th Streets, creating a pedestrian plaza that culminates in the tkts grandstand at the
north end. A master plan for the plaza by the Norwegian architecture
firm Snohetta was completed in 2016, and today the transformation of
Times Square is essentially complete.

❷ Knickerbocker Hotel

1466 Broadway

1901–6 · MARVIN & DAVIS WITH BRUCE PRICE

The Knickerbocker provides a good idea of what a great Broadway hotel
looked like at the turn of the twentieth century. It was a project of John
Jacob Astor IV, who enjoyed a healthy real estate rivalry with his cousin

William Waldorf Astor, developer of the Hotel Astor. The two branches of the family had already developed competing properties on 34th Street where the Waldorf and Astoria hotels sat side by side on what is now the site of the Empire State Building.

When it was completed, the Knickerbocker Hotel boasted elaborately decorated and furnished public spaces and more than five hundred guest rooms. Today the street level has been altered, but the upper stories of the sumptuous facade are intact. The red brick and rich terra-cotta are carefully balanced and accented by limestone ornament inspired by the French Renaissance. The elevation is crowned by a three-story copper mansard roof anchored with pavilions at each corner.

Inside the hotel, Maxfield Parrish's mural *Old King Cole and His Fiddlers Three* once held pride of place in the main bar. Today it can be seen in the King Cole Bar at the St. Regis Hotel on Fifth Avenue. Another major work of art commissioned for the building, Frederic Remington's *The Cavalry Charge,* moved uptown to the Metropolitan Museum in the 1920s when the hotel, suffering from the effects of prohibition, was converted to office and retail use. In 2015 the building was converted once again into a hotel.

⬦ 42nd Street

Ⓐ Bush Tower

130–32 West 42nd Street
1916–18, 1921 · HELMLE &
CORBETT

Harvey Wiley Corbett's classic
skyscraper combines emphatic
verticality, simplified Gothic
detailing, a handsome cathedral-
like portal, and inventive trompe-
l'oeil brickwork. The composition
is topped by a sumptuous crown.
Built as a merchandise showplace,
the thirty-story tower was
designed to attract the attention
of out-of-town buyers. Corbett

intended his building to stand by
itself and carefully detailed all four facades. Today the building is a
bit hemmed in, but you can still enjoy some of its original drama while
taking in the splendid illusionistic effects in the brickwork on the east
facade: those are not real pilasters running up the side of the building.

Across the way, two contemporary buildings occupy the entire north
side of 42nd Street.

Ⓑ Condé Nast Building

4 Times Square
1996–99 · FOX & FOWLE

At street level, the Condé Nast
Building seems to be sheathed
almost completely in electronic
signage. It's worth stepping
back to take in the complex

geometries and varied materials of this intricate 48-story composition with its enormous high-tech rooftop broadcasting mast. The mixture of textures and finishes can at first glance seem chaotic but notice how suavely the architects have rounded the corners at both 42nd and 43rd Streets. Moving east along 42nd Street, the character of the building becomes steadily more sober and less theatrical.

● Bank of America Tower

1 Bryant Park

2004–9 · COOKFOX ARCHITECTS

An understated six-story mid-block wing of this enormous steel-and-glass structure separates it from the Condé Nast Building and provides a smooth transition from the agitated energy of Times Square to the more sedate environment around Bryant Park. To the east the building rises dramatically in angled, crystal-like geometries to a peak at Sixth Avenue. The Condé Nast and Bank of America towers are not only among New York's tallest recent skyscrapers, but also its most energy efficient.

❸ Paramount Theater Building

1501 Broadway

1926–27 · C. W. & GEORGE L. RAPP

The Paramount Building is a flat
slab with dramatic pyramidal
setbacks culminating in a four-
faced clock and an illuminated
globe. At 33 stories, this hybrid
office building and entertainment
palace was, when completed,
the tallest building on Broadway

north of the Woolworth Building. The dramatic arched entrance once
led into the majestic Paramount Theater itself, decorated within an inch
of its life (the lobby was modeled on the chapel at Versailles). After its
career as a film showcase, the 4,000-seat theater was famous as a
home for big band entertainment. Glenn Miller, Tommy Dorsey, Benny
Goodman, and Frank Sinatra all performed here. In 1964 the theater
closed and was converted into offices, but the Paramount name is still
emblazoned above the entrance.

❹ New York Times Building

(Times Annex)

217 West 43rd Street

1912–32 · BUCHMAN & FOX,
LUDLOW & PEABODY, ALBERT
KAHN

The Times annex building
was erected in three stages
between 1912 and 1932 as
the newspaper found itself
perpetually in need of more
space. The new structure by Mortimer Fox mimicked the Italian Gothic
design of the original Times Tower. Much of the building's current
character, however, is derived from the French Renaissance attic and
tower added in 1922 by Ludlow & Peabody. In 2007 the Times moved
to a new headquarters designed by Renzo Piano on Eighth Avenue and
40th Street.

One Astor Plaza 5 (1515 Broadway) fills the west side of Broadway between 44th and 45th Streets. Equipped with futuristic rooftop wings, the building occupies the site of the old Astor Hotel. Completed in 1972 to the designs of Der Scutt, this was the first of the new towers that now dominate Times Square.

Broadway Theaters

In the early years of the twentieth century, when New York's theater district became established around Times Square, most playhouses were built not on Broadway itself, but on side streets where real estate was less expensive. Theaters, often commissioned by theatrical producers, varied greatly in size from large houses designed for vaudeville and musicals to more intimate settings for straight plays. Today the interior of nearly every surviving theater around Times Square has been landmarked to ensure its preservation. Some of the most notable exteriors, such as that of the Lyceum, are also landmarked.

6 Lyceum Theater

149 West 45th Street
1902–3 · HERTS & TALLANT

The Lyceum is a glorious, overstated Baroque extravaganza, solidly built and fitted out with an undulating marquee. Six robustly detailed and banded Corinthian columns support a richly ornamented entablature. Above is a balcony with pedimented windows and a tall mansard roof. The theater was designed to the specifications of producer Daniel Frohman and included not only the auditorium, but rehearsal areas, paint and scenery shops, offices, and an apartment for Frohman himself. Inside, the Lyceum feels lush and intimate with

its two balconies and total seating capacity of under 1,000. This is the oldest operating Broadway theater.

Later in his life, Henry Herts designed the brick and terra-cotta Shubert and Booth Theaters (1913) along Shubert Alley west of Broadway between 44th and 45th Streets. Neither of these straightforward designs has anything like the verve and personality of the Lyceum.

With World War I, theater building in New York came to a standstill. When peace returned, there was considerable pent-up demand, and the mid-1920s saw a dramatic boom in theater construction. The majority of the new theaters were built by the remarkable Shubert Brothers—Sam, Lee, and Jacob. By 1924 the Shuberts owned thirty New York theaters and controlled half of Broadway's seating capacity. Their architect of choice was Herbert J. Krapp, who began his career in the offices of Herts & Tallant. In such buildings as the Majestic and Broadhurst on 44th Street, and the Plymouth, Royale, Golden, and Imperial along 45th Street, Krapp skillfully mixed and matched architectural styles: a little French classicism, a bit of Robert Adam, some Federal-period America, and a touch of Venice.

❼ Marriott Marquis Hotel

1531–49 Broadway
1981–85 · JOHN PORTMAN JR.

This is a hulking brute of a building, the first of the flashy hotels that now populate Times Square. Enormous flat slabs of rooms (nearly 2,000 in all) to the north and south are separated by a forty-eight-story atrium with glass elevators. There is a revolving restaurant at the top. The hotel entrance is hidden within an uninviting driveway between 45th and 46th Street. The lobby and reception desk are eight floors up, safely isolated from the life of the street. To make up for the fact that construction of the hotel necessitated the demolition of five historic theaters, a new theater was included on the third floor.

❽ I Miller Building

1552 Broadway

1926 · LOUIS H. FRIEDLAND

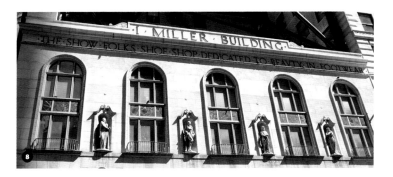

Israel Miller's famous shoe shop is best appreciated from 46th Street. Up at the frieze level is the slogan "The Show Folks Shoe Shop Dedicated to Beauty in Footwear." Just below are tribute statues to a quartet of great actresses: Ethel Barrymore (as Ophelia), Marilyn Miller (as Sunny), Mary Pickford (as Little Lord Fauntleroy), and Rosa Ponselle (as Norma). The choice of America's "four most beloved actresses" was determined by a public poll in the *New York Times*. The statues were executed in 1927 by Alexander Stirling Calder.

On the plaza between Broadway and Seventh Avenue at 46th Street stands a statue of the great composer and performer **George M. Cohan ⑨**. He looks south across Times Square, giving his regards to Broadway. It's the work of George John Lober and dates to 1959.

The plaza stretching north behind the Cohan statue is dominated by a statue of **Father Francis P. Duffy ⑩,** the square's namesake. It is the work of sculptor Charles Keck, erected in 1937. Father Duffy was the larger-than-life chaplain of the overwhelmingly Irish-American 69th Infantry Regiment and saw active service in the Spanish American and First World Wars. After the war, Duffy was the pastor of Holy Cross Church on West 42nd Street where he served a large congregation of theater people.

Just behind the Duffy statue, the all-glass **tkts Booth ⑪,** designed in 2009 by the firm of Perkins Eastman, fills the northern tip of Father Duffy Square. The uptown side is filled with a row of windows offering discounted show tickets. But the real drama is the bright red wedge of **bleachers ⑫** facing south. It's an elegant, clean design. Nearly always packed, the illuminated glass steps provide the perfect perch from which to experience the panorama of Times Square and its signage extravaganza. Great people-watching here, too.

⑬ Palace Theatre

1564 Broadway

1913 · KIRCHHOFF & ROSE

From the day it opened as E.F. Albee's "Valhalla of Vaudeville," everyone wanted to play the Palace. Like many theaters of the era that claimed a Broadway address, the Palace was actually set back on a side street where land costs were lower. The theater presented only a narrow entrance facade to Broadway.

In 1965 to increase revenue, the theater was completely encased in a hotel. Work is currently underway for an even more dramatic transformation. The old hotel is being replaced by a huge new 46-story entertainment and hotel complex that will be wrapped in a vast LED screen. Along the way in a remarkable feat of engineering, the entire landmarked Palace Theater will be raised intact 30 feet to free up street level space for retail use.

At 47th Street, with Times and Duffy Squares behind us, the personality of Broadway begins to change. Electronic signage becomes less exuberant and the pedestrian crush less dense. In the past this stretch was dominated by horse and carriage sales, and then by the automobile business. Until the 1980s nearly every car manufacturer maintained offices and showrooms here. Today only a few reminders of that era remain, mixed in with theatrical and entertainment landmarks.

⑭ The Brill Building

1619 Broadway
1930 · VICTOR BARK JR.

Originally built by developer Abraham Lefcourt, ownership quickly passed to Samuel, Max, and Maurice Brill. From the start, the Brill Building attracted tenants from the music world. It soon became the chosen office location for big band and jazz performers including Tommy Dorsey, Nat King Cole, and Duke Ellington. Music publishers, talent agencies, vocal coaches, and songwriters soon followed. By the 1960s the Brill Building housed more than 160 music-related enterprises, including a nightclub on the second floor. From the final years of Tin Pan Alley to early rock and roll, the Brill Building was the center of the music business in New York.

The art deco building's most notable feature is the elaborate bronze ziggurat that marks the entrance and frames a prominent portrait bust. In all likelihood, it depicts Alan Lefcourt, son of the original owner, who died while the building was under construction. A second portrait of Lefcourt, this time in terra-cotta, crowns the penthouse at the top of the Broadway facade. Don't miss the terra-cotta relief panels marching down the center of that elevation or those between the second and third floors.

⑮ Winter Garden Theater

1634–46 Broadway
1911 · W. ALBERT SWASEY
INTERIOR REMODELED IN 1922 BY HERBERT J. KRAPP

The Winter Garden was originally built by the Vanderbilt family as the American Horse Exchange. As the theater district crept north into the horse and carriage district, this arena was acquired by the Shuberts and converted into a large venue for vaudeville and elaborate revues. While Herbert Krapp redesigned the interior in 1922 to make it more intimate, the building's original equestrian use is still evident in its unusually low and wide auditorium.

16 Hollywood/Mark Hellinger Theater

(Times Square Church)

217 West 51st Street
1929–30 · THOMAS W. LAMB

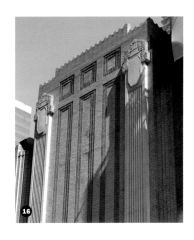

This is one of only two surviving Broadway theaters by Thomas Lamb who designed nearly all the great Times Square movie palaces of the early twentieth century, as well as a large number of sumptuous and exotic neighborhood theaters. The Hollywood Theater is a remarkable blend of art deco on the outside and Hollywood Baroque on the interior. Built as Warner Brothers' New York showcase, the theater has a large stage that enabled it to accommodate both films and live attractions.

17 Hammerstein's Theater

(Ed Sullivan Theater)

1697–99 Broadway
1925–27 · HERBERT J. KRAPP

Producer Arthur Hammerstein commissioned this theater as a memorial to his father, Oscar Hammerstein, the Times Square theatrical pioneer. It is arguably the most luxurious and spirited work by the prolific Herbert J. Krapp. The entryway displays some fine Gothic detailing and handsome polychrome tilework. The once lavish interior featured more of the same, along with stained glass windows flanking the proscenium.

18 Ford Motor Company Building

1710 Broadway
1917 · ALBERT KAHN

Albert Kahn's dignified New York headquarters for the Ford Motor Company combines an understated business-like demeanor with a sunny Mediterranean red-tile roof. Kahn worked mostly in Michigan where he earned an international reputation for his pioneering industrial buildings in cast concrete. He used the same material here, faced in limestone, for this combination showroom and office building. Ford moved out in 1941, and for the next several decades the building was

home to the International Ladies Garment Workers Union (ILGWU).

The Ford Building stands in dramatic contrast to its more exuberant Beaux Arts neighbors: George F. Pelham's **Woodward Hotel** ⑲ (now Dream Hotel) at 210 West 55th Street from 1904 and the **Hotel Carlton** ⑳ (now Albemarle) at 203 West 54th Street of 1903.

㉑ Mutual Life Insurance Building
(MONY Building)

1740 Broadway
1950 · SHREVE, LAMB & HARMON

This stylish tower is the work of Shreve, Lamb & Harmon. It bears more than a passing resemblance both to Rockefeller Center and to the firm's best-known work, the Empire State Building.

For years the MONY building was famous for its illuminated roof mast known as the Weather Star—green star for clear, orange for rain, white for snow. The lights moved upward if the temperature was due to rise; they descended if cold weather was coming. Although the mast no longer prognosticates, the panel at its base still gives the time and temperature.

⬦➲ 57th Street

Perhaps no New York neighborhood is being transformed more rapidly and dramatically than West 57th Street. In the past decade, beginning with buildings such as One57 (157 West 57) and the Steinway Tower (111 West 57), the street has become Billionaires' Row—a string of super-tall skyscrapers with ultra-luxury apartments that command jaw-dropping prices. The buildings literally cast long shadows. They have transformed the Manhattan skyline and altered the character of a neighborhood rich in distinguished historic structures.

Ⓐ Peerless Motor Car and A.T. Demarest Buildings

1758 and 1770 Broadway (224–228 West 57th Street)
1909 · FRANCIS H. KIMBALL

These are two separate buildings, constructed for two different firms, but designed by the same architect and conceived as a stylistic unit. Originally each contained its own automotive show room on the ground floor with repair shops and ware-housing above. Both buildings were acquired and linked in 1918 by General Motors and served as their New York corporate headquarters until 1977.

The larger Peerless Building at the corner extends south until it meets the smaller Demarest Building. The window levels are the same across the two structures, and both are faced in matching matte-white terra-cotta. That said, the buildings are distinguished by subtle differences in their historic detailing. Look for the change halfway along the Broadway facade.

ⓑ Central Park Tower

217 West 57th Street
2014–19 · ADRIAN SMITH+
GORDON GILL

The Central Park Tower is the
tallest residential building in the
world. On 57th Street a dramatic
fluted curtain wall screens a seven-
story foundation building that
houses a new Nordstrom department store and the entrance to the
gigantic residential tower that rises
at the northeast corner of the lot
on 58th Street. The foundation building also includes a wing behind the
landmarked facade of the B.F. Goodrich Building (1909, Howard Van
Doren Shaw and Ward & Willauer) around the corner at 1780 Broadway.

ⓒ American Fine Arts Society
(Art Students League)

215 West 57th Street
1891–92 · HENRY J.
HARDENBERGH

Elegant, formal, and beautifully
balanced, the three-story facade
of this dignified French Renaissance townhouse rises to an
emphatic cornice and a pitched
red-tile roof. The arched entrance
portal to this celebrated art
school is flanked by distinctive
candelabra-like spindles.

Three hundred feet up, the
Central Park Tower cantilevers out to the east over the older building.
The Tower's developers purchased these air rights to ensure that its
residents enjoy unobstructed park views.

🄳 American Society of Civil Engineers Building

218 West 57th Street
1897 · CYRUS L. W. EIDLITZ

Designed as a clubhouse for a professional society, this building is a lovely counterpart to the Art Students League across the street with white glazed brick setting off intricately carved Indiana limestone trim. The window grouping over the main entrance with its ogival arch and framing pilasters is particularly lush.

🄴 Hearst Magazine Building

959 Eighth Avenue
1927–28 · JOSEPH URBAN WITH GEORGE B. POST
2006 · SIR NORMAN FOSTER

The Hearst Building was intended to be both the headquarters of William Randolph Hearst's publishing empire and the anchor for a new commercial and cultural district centered on Columbus Circle.

Florenz Ziegfeld introduced Hearst to Joseph Urban, one of America's great early twentieth-century theatrical designers. His instinct for the dramatic gesture and his keen awareness of art deco and Austrian Secession style are both on display here.

Urban designed his six-story building as the base for an office tower that Hearst hoped to erect at a later date. This plan was finally realized in 2006. Norman Foster's forty-six-story faceted glass tower is as dramatic as the structure from which it rises. Foster designed what was one of the first truly "green" skyscrapers. The triangular framing of the tower required significantly less steel than traditional designs. Inside, a variety of energy-saving innovations have been incorporated, including a three-story glass waterfall in the lobby designed to cool and humidify the space.

West 75th

West 74th

West 73rd

West 72nd

West 71st

22
West 70th
21

West 69th

20

19

West 68th

18 17

16

West 67th

Columbus Avenue

West 66th

13

15

West 65th

Amsterdam Avenue

14

West 64th

12

Broadway →
← Broadway

West 63rd

11

West 62nd

10

West 61st

9

West 60th

8

2

1

Columbus Circle

5

6 7

3

West 58th

4

1 Columbus Circle

3 Time Warner Center

4 Museum of Arts and Design

4 United States Rubber Company Building

5 240 Central Park South

6 Gainsborough Studios

7 220 Central Park South

8 USS Maine National Monument

9 Gulf+Western Plaza

10 15 Central Park West

11 David Rubinstein Atrium

12 Dante Park

13 Richard Tucker Park

14 Lincoln Center

15 Julliard School/Alice Tully Hall

16 Millenium Tower

17 Apple Store

18 Kaufman Center

19 The Copley

20 The Seminole

21 The Ormonde

22 Pythian Temple

Columbus Circle to 70th Street

Columbus Circle ❶ is the site of New York City's zero-mile post— the spot from which distances within and without the metropolis are officially measured. Even without that distinction, the circle would be an important place of convergence and transition. This is where nature and city meet, where commercial Midtown yields to the residential Upper West Side.

When Frederick Law Olmsted and Calvert Vaux laid out Central Park in 1858, they proposed a "Grand Circle" and carriage turn-around for the southwestern corner where Broadway, Eighth Avenue, and Central Park South converge. It took some years, however, before the circle assumed its present form. The key event was the 400th anniversary of Christopher Columbus's landing in the New World.

As 1892 approached, Carlo Barsotti, the dynamic editor and publisher of New York's popular Italian-American newspaper *Il Progresso,* sprang into action. *Il Progresso* was a powerful political force in turn-of-the-century New York, and Barsotti used its pages to advocate for a proper monument to celebrate the achievements of one of Italy's favorite sons. Funds were raised, the 59th Street location secured, and Columbus Circle was created.

The Columbus Monument at the center is the work of Italian sculptor Gaetano Russo. The explorer stands atop a 76-foot rostral column embellished with models of his three ships. (These appear, somewhat confusingly, to be ancient Roman galleys.) The winged figure at the

147

base represents Discovery, and the two bronze plaques below depict Columbus's departure from Spain and his arrival in the New World.

The monument provides a good vantage point from which to consider the challenges of traffic management. Accidents and confusion were endemic here until 1905 when William Eno came up with the novel idea of having traffic move around the circle in only one direction. The modern American traffic circle was born, and incidents declined.

Eno's innovation helped with automotive traffic, but what made Columbus Circle a safe and pleasant place for pedestrians was a major redesign, begun in 2003. The noted landscape firm OLIN added comfortable seating, installed a circular fountain shielded by a landscaped berm, and created clearly marked pedestrian crossing points. Today the center of the circle is a surprisingly quiet and peaceful island in the midst of a churning sea of traffic.

❷ Time Warner Center

10 Columbus Circle
2000–3 · DAVID CHILDS OF
SKIDMORE, OWINGS & MERRILL

This is a fine building on an important site. It closes the vista westward down Central Park South, anchors the southwest corner of Central Park, and marks the start of a new chapter in the story of Broadway as it moves north. The location was once the focus of unsuccessful efforts by William Randolph Hearst to make Columbus Circle a major center for the performing arts. Later, from 1956 to 2000, it was the home of the dreary New York Coliseum, the city's main tradeshow and convention venue. Today the sleek Time Warner Center houses corporate offices, condominiums, a luxury hotel, high-end restaurants, a stylish shopping mall, a supermarket, and three performance spaces for Jazz at Lincoln Center.

Two crisply faceted 55-story towers rise from a base building and central atrium that is carefully curved to follow the outline of the Circle on which it stands. Up above, the towers step back in canted planes to become parallelograms that align both with the Manhattan street grid and with Broadway's path north. Seen from the east, the gap between the two towers admits light and air, making this massive structure seem less overpowering than might otherwise have been the case. The gap also creates the illusion that 59th Street continues unbroken all the way across town. The glass wall of the atrium below perfectly frames the Columbus Column.

❸ Museum of Arts and Design

2 Columbus Circle
1958–64 · EDWARD DURRELL STONE
REDESIGNED 2008 · BRAD CLOEPFIL OF ALLIED WORKS ARCHITECTURE

In 1958 A&P supermarket heir Huntington Hartford hired architect Edward Durrell Stone to build a private museum for his very personal art collection on this awkward but prominent site. The result was an idiosyncratic confection of white marble with filigree decoration, screens of circular harem windows, and a Venetian-inspired arcade that critic Ada Louise Huxtable famously compared to a row of lollipops. Some people found the building surpassingly odd, even silly; others loved it for its eccentricity.

Hartford closed the museum in 1969, and the building went through several owners, including New York City itself. In 2002 the Museum of Arts and Design purchased the building from the city and hired Brad Cloepfil to reconfigure the interior

and apply a new skin. The building is still awkwardly proportioned, the divisions of the facade feel arbitrary, and the gleaming white structure still feels out of place among its neighbors. On the other hand, the interior galleries function well, and the view from the restaurant is spectacular.

❹ United States Rubber Company Building

1790 Broadway
1911-12 · CARRÈRE & HASTINGS

Now called 5 Columbus Circle, but located a block to the south on Broadway, Carrère & Hastings' headquarters for United States Rubber is an elegant Beaux-Arts design. The softly rounded corner at 58th Street links the two facades with their delicate carvings, while continuous vertical piers, broken only at the eighth floor by two horizontal courses, lead the eye upward to a dramatic projecting copper cornice. The building is carefully proportioned, assured, and dignified.

❺ 240 Central Park South

1939–40 · MAYER & WHITTLESEY

This appealing ochre brick apartment building occupies a complex site with elegance and style. As the building's marketing slogan says, this is the place "Where Columbus Circle Meets Central Park." Viewed directly from the Park, the building seems simple and symmetrical. An entry court embellished by Amédée Ozenfant's mosaic *The Quiet City* separates two wings flanking what appears to be a single tower. From Columbus Circle, however, the composition reveals itself to be a set of carefully interrelated towers of differing heights. The wall elevations change too, as do the setbacks. Chimneys, wall slabs, and service enclosures create a lively abstract, almost cubist, composition against the sky.

At street level, a row of shops maintains the lot line, turning the corner and marching diagonally down Broadway in zig-zag fashion. A stylish black band displays the retail signage and the store fronts are handsomely framed in bronze. The roofs of the stores support a private garden extending into the courtyards between the towers. There are gardens on the setbacks and roofs as well.

The apartments are oriented to provide maximum light and air. At the base are wrap-around corner windows. Starting at the seventh floor, the corners are cut away to create terraces set above the tree line of Central Park.

⬤ Gainsborough Studios

222 Central Park South
1907–8 · CHARLES W. BUCKHAM

Artist cooperatives enjoyed a vogue in the early twentieth century, and this is a fine surviving example of these combined living and working spaces. Each studio has a double-height central space with large windows ensuring good northern light. An interior balcony wraps around the studio area to provide sleeping quarters.

The location of the two studios on each floor is clearly demarcated on the facade by distinctive fenestration. A large upper window with vertical lights is supported by two smaller windows flanking a pedimented aedicula filled with stone quatrefoils. Glazed polychrome tiles embellish the top two stories. Over the entrance, a bust of the building's namesake is flanked by Isidore Konti's splendid terra-cotta frieze, "A Festival Procession of the Arts."

⬤ 220 Central Park South

2020 · ROBERT A.M. STERN ARCHITECTS

Stern refers to this handsome 18-story limestone apartment building on Central Park South as a "villa." It fits in comfortably with its older neighbors. The building's real role is to serve as the entrance pavilion for a 950-foot tower placed slightly to the west on 58th Street behind the Gainsborough Studios. There 220 Central Park South sits directly across a narrow street from the even taller Central Park Tower, an unfortunate confrontation of giants.

❽ USS Maine National Monument

1913 · H. VAN BUREN MAGONIGLE
SCULPTURE BY ATTILIO PICCIRILLI

On February 15, 1898, the battleship *Maine* exploded in Havana Harbor, triggering the start of the Spanish-American War. William Randolph Hearst's newspapers had done much to beat the drum for war. He thought a memorial to the

conflict's fallen was essential, and he launched a campaign. It took a while and the location changed several times, but the monument was eventually built.

The central pylon is topped with a brilliantly gilded figure of Columbia Triumphant. At the base of the pylon the battleship sails forth into a fountain complete with an allegorical sculptural group succinctly entitled *The Antebellum State of Mind: Courage Awaiting the Flight of Peace and Fortitude Supporting the Feeble*. Around back is another group, *The Post-Bellum Idea: Justice Receiving Back the Sword Entrusted to War*. The names of the 243 men who died on the Maine are inscribed on the pylon.

Attilio Piccirilli was a member of a celebrated family of stonecutters from Carrara, Italy. They executed Daniel Chester French's portrait of

Lincoln for the Memorial in Washington, D.C., as well as French's Four Continents for the Custom House on Bowling Green. Literally hundreds of well-known monuments around the city are also the family's work.

❾ Gulf+Western Plaza
(Trump International Hotel)

1 Central Park West
1969, THOMAS E. STANLEY
REDESIGNED 1995, PHILIP
JOHNSON

Raised on a podium and intentionally aloof from its surroundings, 1 Central Park West was built as the headquarters of Gulf+Western Corporation. The building housed its offices until it was acquired by Donald Trump in the mid-1990s. He had it stripped to a skeleton, re-clad, and reconfigured as a hotel and condominiums.

The globe in front of the hotel recalls the Unisphere at the 1964 New York World's Fair and signals the location of an expanded entrance to the Columbus Circle subway station. At the foot of the stairs is *Whirls and Twirls,* a colorful ceramic-tile composition by Sol Lewitt; the original tiles from 1904 depicting the largest of the explorer's ships sailing into the station decorate the walls of the IRT number 1 platform.

North of Columbus Circle, Broadway is a different street. The narrow avenue flanked by office towers, stores, lofts, and entertainment venues broadens into a boulevard and becomes the Main Street of a series of primarily residential neighborhoods.

Before the 1880s, the heights along the Hudson River north of 59th Street remained countryside—a series of private estates and small villages (Harsenville, Stryckers Bay,

Bloomingdale Village, Manhattanville, Carmansville). Several events changed all this, bringing about the creation of a new residential neighborhood.

The first was the creation of "The Boulevard." The idea for a major new avenue on the West Side was first proposed by Andrew Haswell Green in 1866. Green chaired the Central Park Commission, the body charged with directing improvements in the entire northern part of Manhattan above 59th Street. To jump start development, Green proposed replacing the meandering old Bloomingdale Road with an American version of the boulevards then being created in Paris. The new tree-lined street would be 150 feet wide with broad flanking sidewalks and a central median.

The Boulevard was to run from what is now Columbus Circle up to 155th Street where the city's street grid ended. Construction began in 1867 just as Boss Tweed was consolidating his political power. Tweed soon gained control of the project and managed to siphon off a good deal of money before the Tweed Ring was broken up. With Tweed's fall, progress on The Boulevard languished.

Development picked up again with the arrival of public transportation. In 1879 the Ninth Avenue Elevated was extended north from 61st Street to 155th, making it possible for potential residents to commute easily to jobs downtown. A building boom followed. Then in 1904 the IRT Broadway line opened, signaling the start of a second wave of residential construction. Hotels, ambitious apartment houses, churches, and neighborhood theaters were quickly built. These attracted a large population of comparatively well-off and sophisticated residents.

Finally, between 1883 and 1890 the city, eager to stimulate development and add a note of distinction to the neighbor- hood, renamed the numbered avenues on the West Side. Eighth Avenue became Central Park West, Ninth Avenue was rechristened Columbus Avenue, Tenth Avenue was changed to Amsterdam, and Eleventh became West End Avenue. The transformation of what had been known as The West End into today's Upper West Side was confirmed in 1898 when The Boulevard was officially renamed Broadway.

⑩ 15 Central Park West

2005–8 · ROBERT A.M. STERN ARCHITECTS

Although it faces Central Park, this luxurious block-filling apartment complex also has a significant presence on Broadway. The two-story retail shopfronts in its limestone base are handsomely framed in bronze and bring a cool dignity to this stretch of the street. Up above, a set-back 35-story tower pivots to align with Central Park West. In terms of massing, materials, and detailing, 15 Central Park West established a model that RAMSA would later follow at 220 Central Park South.

Designers of other apartment buildings in the next several blocks have found their own way to reconcile the city's street grid to the slanting course of Broadway. In each case a six or seven-story base building is topped by a distinctive stepped or slanting tower.

⑪ David Rubinstein Atrium at Lincoln Center

1887 Broadway (61 West 62nd Street)
2009 · TOD WILLIAMS BILLIE TSIEN ARCHITECTS

This narrow, T-shaped passage is a sophisticated and pleasant oasis, a spot to relax and explore the offerings of Lincoln Center nearby. There is a coffee concession as well as comfortable seating, a branch of tkts, a small performance space, and a large digital media wall. Two vertical gardens, a sculptural fountain, large felt paintings by Dutch textile artist Claudy Jonstra, and a golden ceiling pierced by skylights add warmth and texture to the space.

Dante Park ⑫ at 63rd Street, where Broadway and Columbus Avenue intersect, is dominated by Sicilian sculptor Ettore Ximenes's somber bronze figure of the poet. The moving force behind this monument was Carlo Barsotti of *Il Progresso*. Not content with his success in lobbying for the Columbus column, for a statue of Garibaldi in Washington Square, a Verrazano monument in Battery Park, and the creation of Verdi Square at 72nd Street, Barsotti also took on Dante. Initial designs were submitted in 1911, but controversy about the scale of Ximenes's proposed monument and its oversized pedestal caused delays. A compromise was reached, a more modest pedestal by the firm of Warren & Wetmore was designed, and the statue was finally unveiled in 1921 on the 600th anniversary of Dante's death. (To mark another anniversary, the city renamed the corner of 63rd Street and Broadway "Sesame Street" in honor of the celebrated television program's fiftieth birthday.) The "trianguloid" bronze clock at the north end of the park is by Philip Johnson and dates to 1999.

The northern triangle formed by the Broadway/Columbus Avenue intersection occurs at 65th Street. This sliver of pavement with seating shaded by half a dozen London plane trees is **Richard Tucker Park** ⑬, named for the beloved tenor who enjoyed a thirty-year career at the Metropolitan Opera.

⑭ Lincoln Center

One could argue that Lincoln Center and Rockefeller Center are New York's two greatest twentieth-century urban achievements. Rockefeller Center is generally regarded as an unalloyed triumph. Lincoln Center remains in many ways controversial.

By the mid-1950s the tenement neighborhood west of Columbus Avenue, popularly known as San Juan Hill, had been branded as one of the city's worst slums and was targeted for demolition by Robert Moses, then the Chair of the Mayor's Committee on Slum Clearance. Moses's focus on urban renewal coincided with the Metropolitan Opera's increasingly

urgent search for a site on which to build a new theater to replace its dilapidated home on 39th Street.

One thing led to another: partners and politicians were recruited, the project grew, and plans for a centralized performing arts complex— an acropolis— for music, opera, dance, and theater took shape. The bulldozers arrived in 1959, and Philharmonic Hall, the first building of the new Lincoln Center for the Performing Arts, opened in 1962. Additional buildings were added over the next four years. In the decades that followed, Lincoln Center's programs have grown to include film, jazz, chamber music, and outdoor events.

The original core buildings of Lincoln Center included **Philharmonic Hall** (Avery Fisher Hall, now David Geffen Hall; 1962, Max Abramovitz, 1976 renovation, Philip Johnson); **New York State Theater** (now David H. Koch Theater; 1964, Philip Johnson); **Vivian Beaumont Theater** (now Lincoln Center Theater; 1965, Eero Saarinen with later expansions, including a roof-top theater in 2012 by Hugh Hardy); **Library and Museum of the Performing Arts** (1965, Skidmore, Owings, & Merrill; renovated 2001); **Metropolitan Opera House** (1966, Wallace K. Harrison with lobby murals by Marc Chagall)

Many adjectives have been applied to the style of these buildings: classic, modern, timid, pretentious, elegant, vulgar, dignified, reactionary. There is some truth in each of these assessments. The abstracted classical style of the three main theaters with their cool arcades and loggias, each faced in the same travertine (so ubiquitous a material in 1960s Manhattan) makes them seem aloof, official, and corporate.

The model for the layout of Lincoln Center's main theaters was Michelangelo's Campidoglio in Rome: three classical travertine-clad

buildings arranged around a piazza set above the city. Like the Campidoglio or the Acropolis in Athens, the original plan for Lincoln Center elevated the activities there, separating them from everyday life on the streets nearby.

A good deal of Lincoln Center's outdoor magic today is the result of an ambitious renovation undertaken in 2006 by a consortium of architects headed by Diller Scofido + Renfro. To a very significant degree, their work reconnected the originally isolated plaza with the surrounding city, inviting people in. Lively electronic graphics, summertime kiosks, new seating areas, and improved dining options all make the plaza more welcoming and user-friendly. Perhaps the best place to savor Lincoln Center is from the raised grove of trees in Hearst Plaza just north of the opera house. There is a lovely view over the reflecting pool and its Henry Moore sculpture to the torqued slope of the grass roof on the restaurant. The main plaza is particularly dramatic at night when the glass-fronted theaters glow with interior light, patrons crowd the balconies, and visitors gather around the central fountain to share the pleasure of a great urban environment.

The creation of Lincoln Center required the demolition of a vibrant old neighborhood. The Center's success has been the catalyst for the rise of a new and fashionable residential district. If you stand in the plaza today, there are tall new apartment houses everywhere you look. The design of most of the towers may be conventional, but their proximity to the Center keeps them at full occupancy. The neighborhood has become not just a cultural mecca but an attractive place, at least for the well-to-do, to shop, dine, and live.

⓯ Julliard School/Alice Tully Hall

60 Lincoln Center Plaza (Broadway and 65th Street)
1966–68, PIETRO BELLUSCHI
2009, DILLER SCOFIDIO + RENFRO

Belluschi's original building for Julliard, set apart from the plaza across 65th Street, was the boldest and most uncompromising in the Lincoln Center complex: a brooding self-contained Brutalist box, albeit a carefully detailed one. The 2009 renovation changed all of that, adding theatrical drama while ingeniously opening the building to its surroundings and to the life of the street.

The most dramatic changes took place at the Broadway end. The architects sliced out a huge wedge of masonry and cantilevered the upper stories over the sidewalk. The new glass facade glows welcomingly at night and allows tantalizing views inside. At street level the dramatic, thrusting wedge of the cantilever creates a sheltered space for stepped outdoor seating.

As you continue north, notice the trees, shrubbery, seasonal plantings, and corner benches that fill the medians and do so much to maintain Broadway's boulevard character. These amenities are maintained by the non-profit Broadway Mall Association.

Filling the entire block between 67th and 68th Street on the east side of Broadway, the **Millenium Tower** ⓰ (1994, Kohn Pedersen Fox) includes not just high-end apartments, but a 12-screen movie complex, a health club, post office, and retail. Executed in a textured mix of orange, red, and charcoal brick, the Columbus Avenue facade is enlivened by *Dichoic Light Field*, an installation by James Carpenter.

Across the street at 1981 Broadway the **Apple Store** ⓱ (2009, Bohlin Cywinski Jackson) is all sleek transparency on Broadway and solid masonry along the side street. Next door is the **Kaufman Center, Merkin Concert Hall** ⓲ (129 West 67th Street, 1978, Ashok Bhavani; remodeled 2008, Robert A.M. Stern Architects). The facade displays an arresting interplay of raw concrete and brick against the suspended constructivist grid of glass and aluminum panels. Inside there is an attractively spare auditorium along with music studios and classrooms.

At the next corner, **The Copley** ⓳ (2000 Broadway, 1987, Davis,

Brody & Associates) is a meditation on the calming effects of alternating horizontal bands of glass and tan brick.

At 2020 Broadway is **The Seminole** ❷⓪ (1895–96, Ware & Styne-Harde), complete with an entry framed by polished granite columns and surmounted by heraldic shields and guardian lions. The building is an upscale tenement in yellow brick of a sort we shall encounter frequently as we move north.

Next door, the **Ormonde** ❷① (154 West 70th Street, 1889, Robert Maynicke) is a thoughtful neighbor. Matching materials and decorative detailing on the lower floors provide visual continuity along Broadway. At the fifth floor, the Ormonde expresses itself more assertively with a row of pedimented windows and a group of balconies. These bolder features acknowledge the building's greater height and more upscale tone.

❷② Pythian Temple

135 West 70th Street
1927 · THOMAS W. LAMB
CONVERTED TO RESIDENTIAL
USE 1986

The Knights of Pythias, a fraternal organization with a membership of nearly one million in the 1920s, commissioned theater architect Thomas Lamb to build a Manhattan headquarters. Lamb responded with panache, somehow managing, as only he could, to combine ancient Egypt and Babylon (via Hollywood) with art deco. Inside, facilities included a theater, a gym, a bowling alley, and numerous club rooms.

When the Pythians moved out in the 1940s, Decca Records moved in; the building served for several decades as a recording studio. When the Temple was converted to apartments, the solid decorative brick of the original facade was opened up with reflective glass. Fortunately, much of the wonderful exterior terra-cotta survives, including colorful griffins supporting the Pythian shield over the entry, Assyrian capitals to either side, and winged lions on the flanking pavilions. It's hard to get a view of the amazing upper floors, complete with four seated polychrome pharaohs, but do crane your neck.

The Pythian's exuberant decorative scheme may have inspired the bizarre creatures on the marquee of The Coronado at the corner of Broadway and 70th Street (1990, Schumann, Lichtenstein, Claman & Efron).

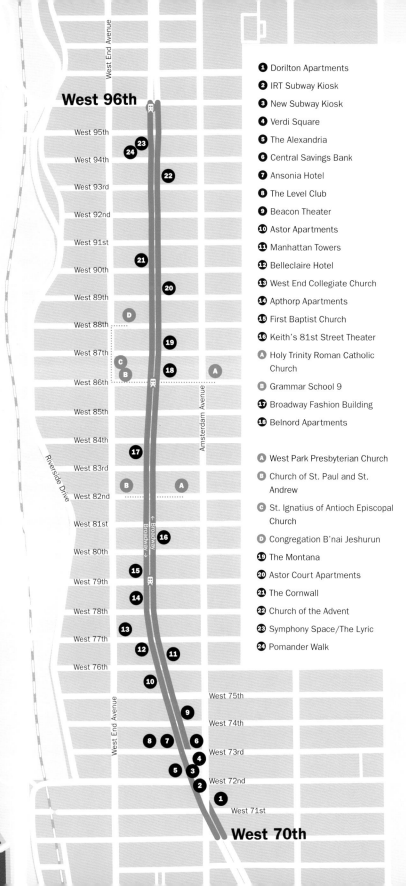

West 96th

West 95th

West 94th

West 93rd

West 92nd

West 91st

West 90th

West 89th

West 88th

West 87th

West 86th

West 85th

West 84th

West 83rd

West 82nd

West 81st

West 80th

West 79th

West 78th

West 77th

West 76th

West 75th

West 74th

West 73rd

West 72nd

West 71st

West 70th

West End Avenue

Amsterdam Avenue

Riverside Drive

Broadway

❶ Dorilton Apartments

❷ IRT Subway Kiosk

❸ New Subway Kiosk

❹ Verdi Square

❺ The Alexandria

❻ Central Savings Bank

❼ Ansonia Hotel

❽ The Level Club

❾ Beacon Theater

❿ Astor Apartments

⓫ Manhattan Towers

⓬ Belleclaire Hotel

⓭ West End Collegiate Church

⓮ Apthorp Apartments

⓯ First Baptist Church

⓰ Keith's 81st Street Theater

Ⓐ Holy Trinity Roman Catholic Church

Ⓑ Grammar School 9

⓱ Broadway Fashion Building

⓲ Belnord Apartments

Ⓐ West Park Presbyterian Church

Ⓑ Church of St. Paul and St. Andrew

Ⓒ St. Ignatius of Antioch Episcopal Church

Ⓓ Congregation B'nai Jeshurun

⓳ The Montana

⓴ Astor Court Apartments

㉑ The Cornwall

㉒ Church of the Advent

㉓ Symphony Space/The Lyric

㉔ Pomander Walk

70th Street to 96th Street

North of Lincoln Center lies the Upper West Side, a neighborhood of residences and their varied and related services. After the Civil War, as was nearly always the case, real estate development here arrived on the heels of public transportation. Columbus Avenue (because of the El) and Amsterdam Avenue (with its streetcars) developed first. The avenues were flanked by rows of standard five-story tenements. More upscale single-family houses clustered on the quieter side streets. By the 1880s, however, apartment living was becoming an increasingly acceptable residential alternative for merchant and professional families, and "French Flats" began to appear. Elaborate apartment buildings and residential hotels arrived first along Broadway and then later along West End Avenue and Central Park West. Not surprisingly, many of the largest and most prestigious buildings built after 1900 were close to the main subway stops at 72nd, 79th, and 86th Streets, making it easy for residents to commute to jobs downtown.

Many of the great buildings in the neighborhood date from the period 1885 to 1910, when even the very rich had embraced the idea of apartment living. New construction slowed during World War I and stopped completely after the stock market crash in 1929. Development did not pick up again until the 1980s, which means that many of the great apartment houses and apartment hotels survived mid-century urban renewal and demolition.

Broadway crosses Amsterdam Avenue at 70th Street, forming Sherman Square, a tiny triangle named for the famous Civil War general. This is a good spot from which to view the truly remarkable building at the corner of Broadway and West 71st Street.

❶ Dorilton Apartments

171 West 71st Street

1900–1902 · JANES & LEO

This gloriously over-the-top Broadway apartment house was erected early in the twentieth century in anticipation of the arrival of the subway. Like others of its type, it was designed to make apartment living not just acceptable, but glamorous and luxurious.

The architectural vocabulary is Parisian Second Empire on steroids. Everything is bolder and brassier than in France. The deeply rusticated limestone base gives way to a red brick mid-section by way of a striped transitional story. Ornament on the central block becomes increasingly riotous as it moves upward to the magnificent slate and copper mansard. Along the way are brackets, quoins, bays, cartouches, statuary, and dormers, all executed with irrepressible vigor.

At the entry court on 71st Street, bronze gates flank a central portal crowned by a heraldic cartouche featuring two putti supporting a shield inscribed with a big D. The flanking columns are topped with improbably over-scaled stone spheres. At the ninth floor there is a great arch tying together the two wings of the building. The arch turns a light well into a stately entry courtyard.

❷ IRT Subway Kiosk

72nd Street between Broadway and Amsterdam Avenue

1904 · HEINS & LA FARGE

Sitting on a tiny island surrounded by traffic is one of only three surviving ticket control houses of the six originally built along the IRT line. At most stations, passengers entered not through a masonry building, but down covered iron stairways. All of these have been lost, but one has been recreated at Astor Place.

The architects of the IRT kiosks had already won the 1891 competition to design the Cathedral of St. John the Divine in Morningside Heights and were actively at work on major buildings for the Bronx Zoo. As was the case at the Zoo, the kiosk commission required Heins & La Farge to create an appropriate style for a new kind of building, one for which there were few historic prototypes. Their solution was a loosely Netherlandish confection of buff brick and limestone, a reminder of Manhattan's Dutch heritage. Like a traditional church facade, there is a high central "nave" accessed through doors at both the north and south. The central hall is flanked by lower "aisles" covering stairs that lead down to the tracks below. The building is an appealing blend of utility and charm, somewhere between a shed and a chapel. The bright "72" in terra-cotta over the entry beckons passengers.

After nearly one hundred years of service, passenger volume had overwhelmed the capacity of the original kiosk. Expansion was in order, but the existing traffic island could not accommodate an additional building. The solution was to close the northbound lane of Broadway from 71st to 73rd Street to enlarge the existing triangular park.

165

❸ New Subway Kiosk

1999–2004 · GRUZEN SAMTON AND RICHARD DATTNER & ASSOCIATES

The new kiosk relieved the overcrowding by adding staircases and elevators. Down below, the tracks were realigned to permit platform expansion. Passengers can now transfer not only from express to local trains, but also from uptown to downtown service.

The design of the new kiosk is respectful of its elder sibling, echoing its overall form in steel, glass block, and ochre brick. Inside is a central hall with a shimmering glass mosaic ceiling by Robert Hickman.

❹ Verdi Square

Broadway/Amsterdam from
72nd to 73rd Streets
1906

Verdi Square was the result of another civic campaign by Carlo Barsotti of *Il Progresso Italo-Americano*. Thanks to his advocacy, the park was named for the celebrated composer, and a monument by Pasquale Civiletti was erected in his honor. The figures on the four sides depict characters from Verdi's operas: Aida, Falstaff, Otello, and Leonora from *La Forza del Destino*.

During the 1960s and 1970s, this now-lovely oasis was the notorious Needle Park of drug dealing legend. Verdi Square was significantly enlarged and re-landscaped in 2003 in conjunction with the construction of the new IRT subway kiosk.

❺ The Alexandria

201 West 72nd Street
1990 · FRANK WILLIAMS AND
SKIDMORE, OWINGS & MERRILL

As they planned this building, the architects clearly had the famous Ansonia apartments one block north very much in mind. The Alexandria's overall massing and rooftop turret happily mirror those of the older building.

The decorative detailing is another matter. Where the Ansonia is consistently bold and assertive in both form and embellishment, here at the Alexandria the decoration is a pallid afterthought. The building's name evokes ancient Egypt, but we are offered only a few lotus capitals on the ground floor pilasters, the balcony railings, and on the crowning "lighthouse."

❻ Central Savings Bank
(Apple Bank for Savings)

2100 Broadway
1926–28 · YORK & SAWYER

This self-assured Florentine palazzo stands in splen-
did isolation on its prominent site, a solid anchor for this section of Broadway.

Boldly rusticated lower floors transition two-thirds of the way up to what is essentially a glazed loggia. Higher still, a projecting cornice supports an additional attic floor and a deep-red tile roof. Notice how the fenestration becomes lighter and more open as the building rises. These upper floors were designed as rental spaces, visually and functionally distinct from the bank below.

Because of site constraints, the building is trapezoidal in plan. When viewed from the south, the east and west facades recede at different angles, causing the building to appear unbalanced. A ceremonial portal complete with clock and winged griffins dominates the south facade. Additional arched windows on the east and west sides admit light into the majestic banking hall with its vaulted and coffered ceiling, elegant stonework, and polished marble floor. The virtuoso ironwork and chandeliers are by Samuel Yellin.

❼ Ansonia Hotel

2101–19 Broadway
1899–1904 · PAUL E. M. DUBOY

With more than 300 units, the Ansonia was, at the time of its construction, the largest apartment hotel in the world. In Paris, such a building would have topped out at six or seven stories; here there

are seventeen. Because the building is just north of Verdi Square where Broadway angles slightly to the east, the Ansonia (which would stand out in any setting) is a true urban landmark, visible in all its splendor from both north and south.

There are wonderful corner towers on Broadway, impressive even without their original cupolas. These were removed, along with the copper cornices, in 1942 to provide material for the war effort. Each side of the building has a design and rhythm all its own. Walk around and take a look at the intricate interplay of the over-scaled carving of the stonework, the delicacy of the iron balcony rails, and the relieving flatness of the brick. All the elements come together into a rich, sumptuous, and surprisingly well-balanced whole.

The Ansonia was built by William Earl Dodge Stokes, an heir to the Phelps, Dodge mining fortune. A major developer on the Upper West Side, Stokes envisioned the Ansonia as his masterpiece. He insisted on fireproof construction, installed special custom-made elevators for both passengers and freight, and even provided rudimentary air conditioning. There was an in-house telephone exchange and a pneumatic-tube message system. Residents could enjoy two swimming pools, a roof garden, and a variety of restaurants and shops. A specially assembled art collection enhanced the common spaces. City electric lines had only recently been installed in the neighborhood, and power was unreliable. An in-house generator ensured that the lights stayed on and the elevators did not stop running. As a further amenity the eccentric Stokes at one time kept chickens and goats on the roof. He sold the eggs to residents.

Due to its solid construction, the Ansonia was an ideal residence for practicing musicians. It was at various times home to Feodor Chaliapin, Ezio Pinza, Yehudi Menuhin, Lily Pons, Gustav Mahler, and Arturo Toscanini. Florenz Ziegfeld, Babe Ruth, and Jack Dempsey were also tenants. During the late 1960s and early 1970s the musical focus changed. One of the Ansonia's former swimming pools became the home of the Continental Baths, a famous gay bath house where Bette Midler launched her career.

❽ The Level Club

253 West 73rd Street
1926–27 · CLINTON & RUSSELL

The Level Club, immediately west of the Ansonia, was designed as the New York headquarters of the Freemasons, incorporating dining rooms, meeting areas, social spaces, a 1,500-seat theater, a billiard room, a full gym and pool, and 285 hotel rooms for visiting Masons. The seventeen-story building was modeled on a conjectural reconstruction of King Solomon's Temple in Jerusalem, an important touchstone in Freemasonry.

The facade is ornamented with a full range of masonic symbols: hexagrams, beehives, all-seeing eyes, levels, trowels, and hourglasses. At the center is a pair of abstracted engaged Corinthian columns crowned with bronze spheres. The columns are supported by corbels representing Hiram Abiff (a character from Masonic legend) and King Solomon. Inside, the two-story lobby is a Venetian Gothic fantasy.

Unfortunately for the Masons, their project was overly ambitious. The Level Club became a public hotel and subsequently the home of Phoenix House, a drug rehabilitation organization. Scenes from the film *Midnight Cowboy* were shot here. Today renovation has given the building new life as a condominium.

9

❾ Beacon Theater

2124 Broadway

1927–28 · WALTER W. AHLSCHLAGER

The 2,900-seat Beacon was initially conceived as a luxurious uptown counterpart to "Roxy" Rothafel's eponymous theater in Midtown. Financing proved problematic and plans changed. The Beacon Theater finally opened in 1929 as a Warner Brothers showcase. Film showings continued until 1974, when the Beacon became what it is today: a premier venue for live music.

To enhance its income, the theater was designed as a component of a larger apartment/hotel complex. The exterior is nondescript, but the interior of the theater more than compensates. Beyond the bronze ticket kiosk, a low vestibule gives way to a soaring oval lobby in loosely classical style. Gold and marble abound, setting off an expansive arcadian landscape mural by Danish artist Valdemar Kjoldgaard. The auditorium itself evokes the tent of a Hollywood sheik. The coffered ceiling is painted to recall fabric; and a plaster drape, decorated with sunburst motifs and supported by tent poles, extends out from the proscenium. A thirty-foot aluminum chandelier dominates the center of the ceiling. Wall murals, also by Kjoldgaard, depict desert caravan scenes. Closer to the stage, the inspiration for the décor switches to the classical world. The highlights are a pair of enormous Grecian goddesses flanking and guarding the proscenium. The entire interior was beautifully restored in 2009.

❿ Astor Apartments

2141–57 Broadway
1905 · CLINTON & RUSSELL
1914 · PEABODY, WILSON & BROWN

The Astor family owned sizable
chunks of real estate on the
Upper West Side. In addition to
numerous cross-street row
houses, they built some of the
most impressive apartment blocks along Broadway.

   The contrast between the sober restraint of the Astor Apartments
and the flamboyant excess of the Ansonia could not be greater.
Here understated gray brick is laid in distinct courses, separated by
recessed horizontal bands and accented with crisp limestone trim.
To dress things up a little, the architects added a few judiciously
placed Italian balconies and a series of oriel windows to the carefully
symmetrical facades. A handsome copper cornice completes the
effect. The original design included just the two southern wings.
Unfortunately, the 1914 addition of a third larger block to the
north, studiously detailed to match the earlier building, disrupts the
compositional balance of the overall group.

⓫ Manhattan Towers/Manhattan Congregational Church

2166 Broadway
1928 · TILLION & TILLION

In 1926 the Manhattan Congregational Church embraced a growing
vogue for "skyscraper churches" and undertook to replace its existing
home with a new 23-story tower. In addition to an 800-seat sanctuary
complete with groined ceiling and stained glass, the building included a
626-room hotel. The hotel failed during the Depression, and the building
was sold for a fraction of its $2.1 million cost. Today the original sanc-
tuary is a theater, and the building is an apartment house called The
Opera. Much of the original gothic decoration has vanished from the facade, but enough remains to suggest the building's ecclesiastical past.

⓬ Belleclaire Hotel

250 West 77th Street

1901–3 · EMERY ROTH OF STEIN, COHEN & ROTH

This is an early work by Emery Roth, who went on to design some of the most famous New York apartment houses of the 1920s and 1930s. For this apartment hotel, his first major commission, Roth created a design that was both traditional and contemporary. While embracing the same basic Beaux-Arts design and planning principles as the architects of the Ansonia and Dorilton, Roth drew on the latest trends in European design—art nouveau and the stylized classicism of the Vienna Secession—for his decorative detailing.

On the Broadway side, two pairs of stone pilasters pass behind an intermediate cornice just beneath the ninth floor. Each pair joins to form an arch at the roof line.

Along the way the pilasters are embellished with spirited Secession-inspired swags. Vienna is also the inspiration for the unusual twelve-over-three glazing pattern of the windows. The cupola that originally topped the round corner tower has disappeared, and the light court on 77th Street has been enclosed to create a lobby for the hotel. The original entry on Broadway, long occupied by store fronts, has been reopened.

⓭ West End Collegiate Church

245 West 77th Street

1891–93 · ROBERT W. GIBSON

This is the current home of one of Manhattan's oldest congregations, an American branch of the Dutch Reformed Church. It should come as no surprise that in creating this picturesque group the architect chose to evoke the Netherlands. Gibson's specific model was secular: the seventeenth-century butchers' guild hall in Haarlem.

Orange roman brick, vigorous stone and terra-cotta trim, and a bright red tile roof enrich a "campus" of informally linked buildings to house the church, school, and parish offices. The building bristles with stepped gables, dormers, and assorted towers, all working together to create a warmly colored, richly textured, and very

satisfying composition. Inside, the bright, open nave features a timber roof and impressive stained-glass windows, three of which are from Tiffany Studios.

⑭ Apthorp Apartments

2209 Broadway
1906–8 · CLINTON & RUSSELL

This block-filling Renaissance palazzo, named for Charles Apthorp who once owned a substantial farm nearby, is another project of the Astor family. The architects are once again Clinton & Russell. Originally there were 104 very large apartments in the twelve-story building along with a fully staffed laundry, servants' rooms, guest apartments, and a rooftop promenade.

On the Broadway facade, carved figures of the Four Seasons stand atop pilasters flanking the soaring entry portal. At street level, beautiful wrought-iron gates are surmounted by "Apthorp" in bold, gilded letters. Visitors and residents pass through this portal, or through a matching one on West End Avenue, into an elegantly landscaped central courtyard. Access to individual apartments is through doorways in each of the courtyard's four corners. Another entrance on 79th Street leads down a ramp to a service area beneath the courtyard.

Seen from the street, the Apthorp is certainly grand. Aware of its potentially overwhelming impact, the architects worked to minimize the mass of the building by carefully organizing its facades. Each elevation is divided both vertically and horizontally into clear bands and topped by a sheltering cornice introduced by refined and beautifully carved garlands.

⑮ First Baptist Church

265 West 79th Street
1894 · GEORGE KEISTER

Set at a diagonal to the street grid, the church presents a powerful asymmetrical facade to this busy corner. Stylistically eclectic and appealingly awkward, the elevation blends the Romanesque and Byzantine with a variety of classical motifs.

Symbolism is embedded in every aspect of the design. The taller tower was once topped with an illuminated beacon representing Christ as the Light of the World. The shorter tower, which was deliberately designed to look unfinished, signals the incomplete nature of the Church, pending Christ's return. The smaller flanking towers with the conical roofs represent the Old (smaller) and New (larger) Testaments. The dates on the facade reference the founding of the congregation and the completion of the present church.

⑯ Keith's 81st Street Theater

2250 Broadway
1914 · THOMAS W. LAMB
CONVERTED 1988, BEYER BLINDER BELLE

This part of Broadway was once lined with movie and vaudeville palaces. Nearly all are gone now, victims of rising land prices and changing leisure preferences. All that remains of this once lavishly ornamented bastion of popular entertainment is the entrance pavilion. It may house an office supply store today, but the theatrical masks on the frieze and at the apex of the arches still hint at its original role.

⟁ 82nd Street

ⓐ Holy Trinity Roman Catholic Church

207 West 82nd Street

1900 · JOSEPH H. MCGUIRE

RECTORY, 1928 BY THOMAS DUNN

Byzantium comes to the Upper West Side. McGuire's building is compact in form and intense in expression. The richly detailed central portal is an intricate puzzle of arches, niches, columns, and circles arranged around a rose window. Both of the twin towers, vigorously striped in red brick and pink terra-cotta, were once topped with Byzantine domes. The facade may be shallow in relief, but it is packed with a pent-up energy that is only partially released by the open arcade at the top.

Inside, Holy Trinity's nave is a dramatic and mysterious space. The great central hall was designed to recall Hagia Sophia, which had deeply impressed the church's pastor on a trip to Turkey. Overhead, the huge dome, constructed of Guastavino tile, leaps up from four tiled pendentives. Beneath the entablature the walls incorporate polychromed terra-cotta, cast bronze, and twenty-eight shades of polished marble. There are more than 100 glowing stained-glass windows grouped by ecclesiastical themes. With the exception of the circular rose window at the back of the nave, all were manufactured in Germany and installed in 1930.

(Note: Mass is celebrated daily at 9:00 and 5:30 and the church is open before and after these services. There are multiple services on Sunday mornings. At other times, accessibility is hard to predict.)

Walk back across Broadway to the corner of 82nd Street and West End Avenue.

❾ Grammar School 9
(Mickey Mantle School)
460 West End Avenue
1894 · C. B. J. SNYDER

This is an early design by the remarkably energetic and influential Superintendent of School Buildings C. B. J. Snyder. Between 1891 to 1923 Snyder built nearly 200 schools in a sustained effort to accommodate New York's exploding population.

To fit into its Dutch-inspired neighborhood, Snyder selected warm, pale brick and included some timid stepped gables and dormer windows of Low Country inspiration. Fireproof materials were used in construction and, as in his other schools, large windows admit plenty of light and air. The building now houses the Mickey Mantle School for children with special educational needs.

⓱ Broadway Fashion Building

2315 Broadway

1930–31 · SUGARMAN & BERGER

Built to attract a high-end retail clientele, this stylish art deco treasure is energetically executed in steel, glass, and glazed black terra-cotta. Expansive windows are separated vertically by dark pilasters culminating in a parapet of abstracted mountain peaks. Beneath the windows there are horizontal metal panels in pale gray embellished with wavy zig-zag patterns. The materials are industrial; the effect is glamorous.

⓲ Belnord Apartments

225 West 86th Street

1908–9 · H. HOBART WEEKES OF HISS & WEEKES

Erected within two years of the Apthorp, this competing luxury apartment building embraces the same central courtyard plan, Renaissance design vocabulary, and enormous scale. If we compare the two buildings, the Belnord's facade is a little busier (note the segmentally arched windows in the center section) and less stylistically assured. Because the entry portals are around the corner on the side street rather than on the avenue, the Broadway facade lacks focus.

⬭ Three Churches and a Synagogue

❶ West Park Presbyterian Church

165 West 86th Street
1889 · HENRY F. KILBURN
INCORPORATING EARLIER WORK
BY LEOPOLD EIDLITZ

The congregation was one of the
first to erect a prominent church
on the developing Upper West
Side. They began on 86th Street with a small chapel by Leopold Eidlitz.
A few years later this was incorporated into a large, bold Romanesque
building by Henry Kilburn. The overall massing is informal and
picturesque with the tall corner tower providing a powerful anchor. The
stonework is heavily rusticated, and the deeply chromatic sandstone
really makes the church stand out. Today the exterior is remarkably
intact. The interior, used both for worship services and as a venue for
performing arts events, shows a good deal more wear.

❷ Church of St. Paul and St. Andrew

540 West End Avenue
1895–97 · R. H. ROBERTSON

On West End Avenue, each of the church's three portals is flanked by
colossal Corinthian pilasters. Above each entry is an oculus, bracketed
by carved standing angels. A strong triangular pediment rises above
the clerestory level. What really gives the building its dynamism,
however, are the two towers. To the north is a stocky, square campanile
with a belfry set back slightly at an angle to the facade. The response
on the south side is a deliberately over-scaled octagonal tower that
anchors the whole composition to the street corner. On 86th Street,
the facade unfolds rhythmically along a row of colossal pilasters.

Next door on West End Avenue is **St. Ignatius of Antioch
Episcopal Church ❸,** designed by Charles C. Haight in 1902. The

exterior of St. Ignatius seems closed and fortress-like, but the interior is warm and welcoming. This bastion of Anglo-Catholic worship has the cozy feeling of village church. The walls are faced with courses of thin, carefully laid Roman brick in a soft yellow tone. The ceiling is a classic example of Guastavino tilework. Note as well the fine, bright stained-glass behind the handsome altar.

ⓓ Congregation B'nai Jeshurun

257 West 88th Street

1918 · HENRY B. HERTS AND WALTER SCHNEIDER

When this venerable congregation (founded in 1825) decided to follow its members uptown, they made an interesting choice of designers: theater architect Henry Herts. Both he and Schneider were members of the congregation.

The ornately carved portal leads to a lavish interior, an exotic fantasy. The sanctuary blends motifs from across North Africa and the Middle East into a lush and richly chromatic stage set. A roof collapse in 1991 required a new truss-work ceiling, but the interior retains much of its exotic glamour.

⓳ The Montana

247 West 87th Street

1986 · GRUZEN PARTNERSHIP

Here is a nod to the classic twin-towered buildings of Central Park West, although without the park to overlook. The building is a good neighbor. The main block conscientiously maintains the roof line and fenestration rhythms of the apartments to its north and south. The brick color above and the limestone masonry at street level are also well integrated with the buildings to either side.

⓴ Astor Court Apartments

205 West 89th Street

1914–16 · CHARLES A. PLATT

Like other properties developed by the family, Astor Court is dignified and understated. Its

entrance is tucked discreetly around the corner on 89th Street away from the bustle of Broadway. Unlike the Apthorp, the Astor Court fills only half the block. As a result, the internal courtyard is U-shaped, and its garden is pleasantly intimate. The most distinctive architectural feature is the splendid floating cornice that seems to hover effortlessly above the attic story.

㉑ The Cornwall

255 West 90th Street

1909–10 · NEVILLE & BAGGE

This is the first work we have seen by the firm of Neville & Bagge, whose apartment and tenement buildings will dominate stretches of Broadway farther north in Hamilton Heights. Between 1900 and 1917 the firm filed plans for more than 400 buildings. Their formula is remarkably consistent: stone base, brick mid-section, and an exuberant, wildly eclectic decorative crown.

㉒ Church of the Advent

2502 Broadway
1900 · WILLIAM A. POTTER

This highly distinctive church is the work of William A. Potter, one of New York's great advocates for English High Victorian design. The exterior elevation is spikey and asymmetrical with strongly contrasting stone trim around the brickwork. The short pilaster at the corner is a fascinating and deliberately awkward solution to the challenge of anchoring a visually important spot.

The interior decoration of the elevated sanctuary is largely the work of Tiffany Studios. There are stained-glass windows, a finely detailed ceramic and mosaic reredos, an equally beautiful pulpit and lectern, and distinctive hanging lanterns.

㉓ Symphony Space/ The Lyric

2537 Broadway
1915
THEATER RENOVATIONS, 2002,
POLSHEK PARTNERSHIP
APARTMENT BUILDING, 2001–2,
COSTAS KONDYLIS & PARTNERS

This site has a complex history. In 1915 Vincent Astor opened an ambitious food-and-fish market here. The venture was not a success, so in 1917 the property was sold to restauranteur and night club owner Thomas Healy. He turned the main floor into an ice skating rink and the lower level into a restaurant. The ice rink only lasted a year, at which point the space was transformed into a theater. Healy's long-term plan was to acquire the entire block all the way to West End Avenue and to erect a hotel. The developer's death and the subsequent Depression brought these ambitious schemes to an end.

In 1931 a small movie theater named the Thalia opened in the former restaurant space. For decades, it was a mecca for film buffs while the main theater upstairs remained shuttered. In 1978, thanks to the efforts of conductor Allan Miller and playwright Isaiah Sheffer, the main theater reopened as Symphony Space. It continues to offer an active program of readings, concerts, films, and live performances. Income from sale of the air rights over the theater allowed Symphony Space to renovate it facilities. The new red brick and limestone apartment building by Costas Kondylis, with its understated art deco detailing and thoughtful massing, succeeds in its intention to fit well within the neighborhood.

㉔ Pomander Walk

261–267 West 94th Street
1921 · KING & CAMPBELL

Just down the hill from Broadway is a charming remnant of Healy's ambitious original project. In 1921, as he worked to assemble the parcels of land needed for his hotel, Healy decided to put the vacant property behind his theater to a somewhat whimsical use. Ten years earlier, he had greatly enjoyed the Broadway play *Pomander Walk* by

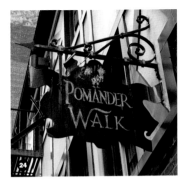

Lewis Parker. Healy commissioned his architect to design a residential complex that recreated the look and feel of the English village street that had been the set for Parker's play. Healy's village includes twenty-eight miniature houses, sixteen of which face onto a raised interior street running north–south in the middle of the block. Originally each house contained two apartments and its own tiny front garden. Although the entire complex is unified by the use of Tudor half-timbering and stucco, each house is subtly different in its architectural detailing. Today Pomander Walk, lovingly maintained by its residents, remains an enchanting world apart.

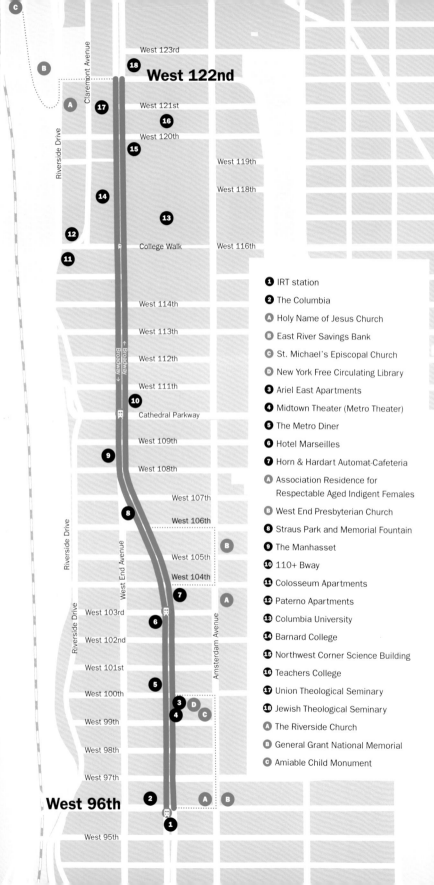

West 122nd

West 123rd
West 121st
West 120th
West 119th
West 118th
West 116th
College Walk
West 114th
West 113th
West 112th
West 111th
Cathedral Parkway
West 109th
West 108th
West 107th
West 106th
West 105th
West 104th
West 103rd
West 102nd
West 101st
West 100th
West 99th
West 98th
West 97th
West 96th
West 95th

Claremont Avenue
Riverside Drive
Broadway
West End Avenue
Riverside Drive
Riverside Drive
Amsterdam Avenue

1 IRT station
2 The Columbia
A Holy Name of Jesus Church
B East River Savings Bank
C St. Michael's Episcopal Church
D New York Free Circulating Library
3 Ariel East Apartments
4 Midtown Theater (Metro Theater)
5 The Metro Diner
6 Hotel Marseilles
7 Horn & Hardart Automat-Cafeteria
A Association Residence for Respectable Aged Indigent Females
B West End Presbyterian Church
8 Straus Park and Memorial Fountain
9 The Manhasset
10 110+ Bway
11 Colosseum Apartments
12 Paterno Apartments
13 Columbia University
14 Barnard College
15 Northwest Corner Science Building
16 Teachers College
17 Union Theological Seminary
18 Jewish Theological Seminary
A The Riverside Church
B General Grant National Memorial
C Amiable Child Monument

96th Street to 122nd Street

This section of our walk takes us to the first of a series of "heights" overlooking the Hudson River, and then down the slope to Manhattanville. Like the Upper West Side, the stretch of Broadway between 96th and 110th Streets, once known as the Bloomingdale Village, is filled with blocks of apartment buildings and tenements. At 104th Street, Broadway angles to the west, keeping to the natural geological ridge line. As it crosses 110th Street, the clustering of apartment blocks becomes denser, reflecting the impact of Columbia University and the other institutions that fill Morningside Heights.

Let's begin with the subway, always a crucial catalyst for Broadway's development. In 2010, the MTA recognized that neighborhood population growth around 96th Street had overwhelmed the existing IRT station. The original entries on the east and west sides of Broadway were closed and replaced with a futuristic **pavilion** ❶ on the central traffic island. A twenty-first century version of the entrance kiosks at 72nd Street, the pavilion provides new staircases and elevators to a major express route station. The well-planted plaza in front offers welcoming seating. As part of the project, the former public restrooms on the median just north of 96th Street were converted into a community art center.

❷ The Columbia

275 West 96th Street
1984 · LIEBMAN WILLIAMS ELLIS

Built on the site of the Riviera-Riverside theater complex, the Columbia was the first of many new apartment houses that rose on Broadway during the 1980s, signaling the area's rebirth as a desirable residential neighborhood. The facade facing Broadway, with its alternating bands of glass and pale brick, is not very interesting, but the tower, set back along 96th Street, bristles with spiky interwoven cantilevered balconies.

❸ Ariel East Apartments

2628 Broadway
2007 · CETRA RUDDY

At thirty-seven stories, it's hard to miss this building (or its companion across Broadway). The stepped design and striking red highlighting of Ariel East make it a handsome urban landmark. It is, however, dramatically out of scale for the neighborhood. Clearly the zoning commission agreed. Shortly after its completion, new regulations were put in place limiting the height of new buildings along Broadway between 96th and 110th Streets to 145 feet.

⬦ Amsterdam Avenue 96th to 100th Street

There are four distinctive buildings just to the east of Broadway that are worth a detour.

Ⓐ Holy Name of Jesus Church

Amsterdam and 96th Street
1898 · T. H. POOLE

Most of the church-goers who settled in row houses on the Upper West Side in the late-nineteenth century belonged to Protestant denominations. When the Holy Name parish was established near this site in 1868, it was the only Roman Catholic Church between Columbus Circle and 131st Street. By the time the present building opened in 1900 the balance had begun to shift as large numbers of Catholic worshippers moved into the tenements and apartment buildings along the avenues.

The crisply detailed exterior is somewhat cold and tight, but the spacious white-and-gold interior with its broad nave, ample transepts, and dark hammer-beam roof is expansive and welcoming.

Across Amsterdam Avenue is Walker & Gillette's handsome **East River Savings Bank** Ⓑ of 1927. Beautifully carved engaged Ionic columns rise straight from the sidewalk, framing double-height windows and supporting a

solid entablature. The quotations on the entablature about education and thrift are from Jefferson, Lincoln, and Roosevelt.

⊙ St. Michael's Episcopal Church

225 West 99th Street
1891 · ROBERT W. GIBSON
PARISH HOUSE (WITH F. CARLES
MERRY) 1896; RECTORY, 1912

St. Michael's Church is an
imposing Romanesque-revival
structure of buff-colored, rough-faced limestone extending along
Amsterdam Avenue and anchored at the corner by a soaring bell tower
of Italian inspiration. An asymmetrical parish house and a restrained
rectory along 99th Street complete the handsome complex

The entry to the church is through an arched portal on Amsterdam
Avenue. The unusually long and tall nave is roofed with a wooden
barrel vault and culminates in a dramatic apsidal chapel with its seven
splendid Tiffany windows and a luxuriant altar. The dramatic color
scheme does much to warm up an interior that could easily seem
cavernous. In 1920 Tiffany Studios returned to the church to design
the Chapel of the Angels with its Gloria mosaic and flanking columns.

⊙ New York Free Circulating Library

206 West 100th Street
1898 · JAMES BROWN LORD

Before there was the New York
Public Library with its extensive
network of neighborhood
branches, there was the private
New York Free Circulating Library.
Supported by Andrew Carnegie,
J. P. Morgan, and Cornelius
Vanderbilt to provide "moral and
intellectual elevation for the masses," the library had outposts around
the city. This branch continued as a library until 1961, when it was sold
to the Ukrainian Academy of Arts and Sciences.

The building, inspired by French eighteenth-century models, is faced
with glazed Roman brick above a rusticated limestone ground floor. The
decoration becomes richer as the building rises.

❹ Midtown Theater

(Metro Theater)

2626 Broadway

1932 · BOAK & PARIS

If Ariel East is representative of
this section of Broadway today,
the Midtown Theater is a reminder
of quieter days. This small art
deco gem is distinguished by
a glazed terra-cotta facade
designed around a polychrome
medallion with stylized figures
and classic masks of Comedy and
Tragedy. Manhattan was once the
home of many small neighborhood
theaters like this one. They were
built during the Depression when
the movie palaces of earlier years
were becoming financially harder
to sustain. In 1934 there were

eighteen historic movie theaters along Broadway between 59th and
110th Streets. Except for the Beacon, all are gone now. All that remains
of the Midtown is the facade.

The **Metro Diner** ❺ (2641 Broadway) occupies the Henry Grimm
Building, one of the first structures built on the new Boulevard in
the late 1860s. Today it is one of only two wooden structures left on
Broadway. Grimm was able to build in wood because at the time the
city's prohibition against frame construction extended only as far north
as 86th Street.

❻ Hotel Marseilles

2689–93 Broadway

1902–5 · HARRY ALLAN JACOBS

The Marseilles is another stately
Beaux-Arts apartment hotel,
this time with an English
Edwardian accent. The rusticated
base, the red brick midsection

tied with stone quoins, and the sloping mansard roof punctuated with dormers are all familiar. The architectural elements are bold, but under English influence, the massing is simplified and the detailing considerably less florid than at the Ansonia and Dorilton. Around the corner on 103rd Street distinctive pairs of banded and fluted columns flank the entrance.

❼ Horn & Hardart Automat-Cafeteria

2710 Broadway

1930 · F. P. PLATT AND BROTHER

The first Automat in New York was an instant success when it opened in 1912. Who could resist the gleaming porcelain wall of cubby holes, each holding a different treat? Customers would drop nickels in the slot and turn the beautiful brass knob. The small glass-fronted door would then pop open allowing them to retrieve their purchases. This branch opened in 1930 and continued to serve patrons until 1953.

   Horn & Hardart may be gone, but the building with its distinctive terra-cotta panels and stylized capitals remains. The architects carried out a good deal of work for the company, creating a standard store design with large windows and art deco details that became an easily recognizable corporate trademark. The terra-cotta here came from the same firm that provided the panels for Cass Gilbert's Broadway Chambers and Woolworth Buildings.

⬥ Richard Morris Hunt

Ⓐ Association Residence for Respectable Aged Indigent Females

891 Amsterdam Avenue
1881 · RICHARD MORRIS HUNT
EXPANDED 1907 BY CHARLES A. RICH

This evocative French-inflected Victorian Gothic structure is a rare survivor of a style Hunt used for institutional buildings in the years following the Civil War. Dark red brick, brownstone trim, restrained polychromy, simple square corner towers, and crisply pointed dormers piercing a mansard roof make this a handsome, if sober, composition.

The Association was founded in 1814 by a group of socially prominent matrons to assist poor women widowed in the Revolution or the War of 1812. The group's initial home was downtown, but like so many other institutions, the Association moved north when additional space was required. Today the building houses a youth hostel.

Ⓑ West End Presbyterian Church

165 West 105th Street
1891 · HENRY F. KILBURN

West End Presbyterian is a close cousin to West Park Presbyterian at 86th Street and Amsterdam Avenue: same denomination and architect, same ground plan, bold massing, and powerful tower. But here Kilburn replaced the dark, deeply rusticated sandstone, with light-gray brick, accented with banding and bright terra-cotta ornament. The detailing is historically eclectic—some Venetian Gothic, some Norman, a bit of the Renaissance.

At 106th Street Broadway curves slightly to the west to align again with the route of the Old Bloomingdale Road from which it has drifted. At 107th Street Broadway intersects with West End Avenue.

❽ Straus Park and Memorial Fountain

Broadway and West 106th Street

1915 · H. AUGUSTUS LUKEMAN, SCULPTOR; EVARTS TRACY, ARCHITECT

When the *Titanic* sank in 1912, Isidor and Ida Straus were among the 1,500 passengers who lost their lives. Straus was the owner of R. H. Macy & Co. He built the firm's flagship store on Herald Square and was a generous philanthropist. The Strauses lived in a frame house nearby on Broadway at 105th Street.

After their deaths, a public subscription was held to raise money for a memorial, and in 1912 the city renamed what had been Schuyler and then Bloomingdale Square in honor of the couple. The memorial fountain and exedra were dedicated on April 15, 1915, three years to the day after the *Titanic* sank. On the exedra is a quotation from the second book of Samuel, "Lovely and pleasant were they in their lives and in their death they were not divided," which commemorates Mrs. Straus's decision to remain on the ship with her husband rather than take her place in a lifeboat.

West of Straus Park, the blocks between 105th and 109th Streets above Riverside Park are particularly handsome ones. There are many substantial rowhouses as well as the Morris and Laurette Schinasi House, a freestanding mansion at the corner of Riverside Drive and West 107th Street. It was designed in 1907 by William Tuthill, the architect of Carnegie Hall.

❾ The Manhasset

2801–2825 Broadway
1899–1901 · JOSEPH WOLF
1901-05 · JANES & LEO

The Manhasset grew over time.
The initial eight floors, fairly
modest in style, went up first.
Only a few years later, the building got an upgrade: three additional
stories, a mansard roof, and some fancy entry portals. The designers
of the expansion were Janes & Leo, who a year earlier had created the
Dorilton at 71st Street.

   The Manhasset is actually two contiguous buildings, one facing
West 108th Street and one facing 109th. The complex was designed
to present a unified face to Broadway, but the fenestration of the
two halves of the facade does not match. This reflects the fact that the
south building was originally laid out with larger apartments.

110th Street/Cathedral Parkway marks the beginning of
Morningside Heights, which sits on a distinct natural plateau
with Broadway as its spine. For much of the nineteenth century,
this was an outlying area dominated by the Bloomingdale
Insane Asylum. In the 1880s, as real estate development
marched northward, the Asylum's trustees began to sell off
parcels of land. The bulk of the property was purchased in
1892 by Columbia University as the site for a new campus.
Other educational, religious, and charitable organizations soon
followed. Today Morningside Heights is filled with institutions:
the Cathedral of St. John the Divine, Riverside Church, Mount
Sinai St. Luke's Hospital, Barnard College, Teacher's College,
two seminaries, and the Manhattan School of Music.

⑩ 110+ Bway
(545 West 110th Street)

2840 Broadway
2007 · PBDW ARCHITECTS

What a pleasure to encounter
a new apartment block that
combines style and modesty.
110+ is light, airy, nicely detailed,
and an all-around good neighbor.
Across the street the combination private school/apartment building
(2003, Beyer Blinder Belle) anchors the southeast corner
with authority.

The next blocks offer an interesting assortment of apartment
houses in a variety of historic
styles. 112th Street provides a
dramatic look eastward to the
facade of the Cathedral of St.
John the Divine. At 116th Street,
the road slopes down sharply to
the west, offering a view of the

Colosseum Apartments ⑪ and
the **Paterno Apartments ⑫** at the corner of Riverside Drive. Both
buildings are by the firm of Schwartz & Gross and date to 1910.
Their sweeping and complementary curves frame the vista to the river
and bring great urban energy to this important junction where 116th
Street, Riverside Drive, and Claremont Avenue converge.
   On the east side of Broadway at 116th Street is the main entrance
gate of Columbia University.

⑬ Columbia University

Broadway between 113th and 120th Streets
1893–1913 · MASTER PLAN AND ORIGINAL BUILDINGS BY CHARLES
FOLLEN MCKIM OF MCKIM, MEAD & WHITE

Founded as Kings College on lower Broadway in 1754, Columbia
College moved north to Madison Avenue and 49th Street in 1857 and

again to Morningside Heights in 1897. College President and later New York City Mayor Seth Low provided the impetus for the relocation and for the evolution of Columbia into what he called a "metrropolitan university." He pressed the trustees to acquire the site of the former Bloomingdale Asylum and supervised an extended process that ended with the selection of McKim as the architect of the new campus. Low and McKim shared a vision for Columbia as an educational institution fully engaged with the life of the city.

McKim's campus plan embodied the ideas of the prevailing City Beautiful movement and was inspired by elements of the University of Virginia, the World's Columbian Exposition in Chicago, and by Italian Renaissance visions of an ideal city. Instead of following the Oxford/ Cambridge model for a campus conceived as a closed Gothic cloister, McKim laid out Columbia as a series of free-standing pavilions arranged around open courtyards on an expansive elevated terrace— an academic city on a hill. At the center, facing south, is a monumental classical library. It remains the architectural focus of the Columbia campus.

Low Memorial Library

1895-97 · CHARLES FOLLEN MCKIM OF MCKIM, MEAD & WHITE

Daniel Chester French's majestic *Alma Mater* presides over a broad, gently rising flight of steps that leads to a domed and colonnaded temple of true Roman grandeur. While the spirit of the Pantheon hovers over McKim's design, the building with its Greek cross plan and

13

thermal windows also draws heavily on Italian High Renaissance and French Beaux-Arts models.

The interior of the central rotunda is awe-inspiring. Light pours in through thermal windows to highlight statues of Demosthenes, Euripides, Sophocles, and Julius Caesar. They stand high on balconies supported by columns of green Connemara marble and polished Vermont granite with bronze Ionic capitals. Just behind the central hall is a rectangular room used for history and art displays. It's worth a visit for the exquisitely detailed coffered ceiling.

It's a pleasure to walk around the Columbia campus, particularly the part surrounding Low Library, where the elements of McKim's plan were most fully realized. The sections bounded by Schermerhorn, Avery, Fayerweather, and St. Paul's Chapel come closest to the density he sought. The combination of dark-red pressed brick with vigorous stone trim and richly detailed copper cornices conveys appropriate seriousness of purpose, and together they form an impressive ensemble.

Two buildings in this area merit special attention. **Buell Hall,** just in front and slightly to the east of Low Library, is the only surviving building from the Bloomingdale Asylum. With its elegant brickwork, detailed stone carving, fine green tile roof, and dignified proportions, **St. Paul's Chapel** (1903–7, Howells & Stokes) recalls the High Renaissance architecture of northern Italy, particularly Milan. Inside, a short nave and domed crossing lead to a curved apse with beautiful stained-glass windows by John La Farge. The glass in the large Palladian windows in the transepts by Henry Wynd Young Jr. and J. Gordon Guthrie, is nearly as beautiful. The walls are rich warm Roman brick. Above, a terra-cotta frieze gives way to the rose-and-white herringbone pattern of

13

Guastavino tile pendentives. In the dome, the same tile is arranged in bold concentric rings. The twenty-four small windows around the base of the dome are decorated with the coats of arms of early New York families.

Behind Low Library and just to the east of the massive Uris Business School is the **Sherman Fairchild Center** (1977-97, Mitchell/Giurgula Associates). The abstract patterning of its floating, ceramic-panel facade elegantly closes the vista to the north. At the south end of the campus, just west of Butler Library, Bernard Tschumi's **Lerner Hall Student Center** (1999) embraces and challenges its context. Behind a glass wall facing the campus there is a complex series of circulation ramps. On the other facades the architect has adhered to Columbia's tradition of brick and limestone.

For the next few blocks, Broadway is bounded to the east by the walls of Columbia's inward-looking campus and to the west by those of **Barnard College ⑭.** At 117th Street the main gate frames **Barnard Hall** (1916, Arnold Brunner). Much more interesting are the **Milstein Learning Center** (2017, Skidmore, Owings & Merrill) and **Diana Center** (2010, Weiss/Manfredi), the college's two newest buildings. The rich orange color of the Diana Center with its dramatic fourth-floor glass projection is particularly striking. Inside the campus of the women's college the two buildings carry on a spirited dialogue across the green lawn.

⑮ Northwest Corner Science Building

Broadway and West 120th Street

2009 · RAFAEL MONEO AND DAVIS BRODY BOND AEDAS

The Northwest Corner Building is a crisp, contemporary coda to the main Columbia campus, austere, taut, assured, and filled with energy. The eye-catching pattern of diagonal braces and louvers is not only visually engaging; it reflects some complex engineering challenges. The new building is literally a bridge, suspended over an existing gymnasium.

While the upper floors of the Northwest Corner Building exude a self-contained contemporary independence, the lower floors embrace Columbia's architectural past. The lower levels are clad in soft pinkish marble carved in diagonals, which establishes a textural and coloristic link to McKim's brick and stone. Hovering over the entry at the corner, a glass-walled café faces north toward the university's new campus down the hill in Manhattanville.

⑯ Teachers College

Broadway between 120th and 121st Streets

Founded in 1889, Teachers College is the oldest graduate school of education in the United States. The former **Horace Mann School** (1899, Howells & Stokes and Edgar H. Josselyn) on Broadway is a handsome Victorian blend of brownstone and red brick, enlivened with diaper patterning. To the east on 120th Street are William A. Potter's original college buildings from 1892, in the same English Victorian mode, but striped rather than diapered. The next building, Allen and Collens' **Russell Hall** (1922), is a dry, streamlined essay in collegiate gothic.

Student housing is on 121st Street, with accommodations in **Bancroft Hall** (509 West 121st Street) an early apartment building by Emery Roth (1901–11). Brick, stone, terra-cotta, elaborately detailed copper bay windows, mysterious rooftop aeries, and projecting eaves all contribute to a building full of personality. Next door, at **517 West 121st Street** is a contemporary student residence hall that acknowledges Roth's exuberance with an understated vocabulary.

On the west side of Broadway facing Teacher's College is Union Theological Seminary. Rising behind is the soaring spire of Riverside Church. The Gothic towers of all three institutions were designed by Allen & Collens over a span of twenty years.

⑰ Union Theological Seminary

Broadway between 120th and 122nd Streets
1906 · ALLEN & COLLENS

Founded in 1836, Union Theological is an independent, non-denominational seminary, closely affiliated with Columbia University. The seminary's present campus, opened in 1910, is organized around a central quadrangle that closely recalls the colleges of Oxford and Cambridge.

   The complex is anchored by the Brown Memorial Tower at the corner of Broadway and 120th Street. Massive and restrained, with crisp detailing, the four-square English Perpendicular Gothic tower has two imposing portals. Inside, there is a circular lobby with a richly inlaid floor and elaborate vaulting. The entry to the seminary's library and its important collection is up a complex circular stairway.

⑱ Jewish Theological Seminary

3030 Broadway
1928 · GEHRON, ROSS & ALLEY

This is a strange building. The overall inspiration seems to be Georgian. However, somehow during the design process the style, scale, and detailing became detached from each other, and harmony was never realized. The corner entry tower, built to house the school library, is hugely over-scaled. And it's hard to know what to make of the little balcony up top, projecting in front of what resembles a miniature colonial church. The tower's contemporary fenestration was inserted in what was originally a solid wall of brick after a disastrous fire in 1966.

Riverside Drive

Ⓐ The Riverside Church

490 Riverside Drive
1926–30 · HENRY C. PELTON
WITH ALLEN & COLLENS

This huge interdenominational
church with its 392-foot tower
was commissioned by John D.
Rockefeller Jr. The tower houses
twenty-one floors of church offices
and a seventy-two-bell carillon.
Elsewhere in the complex are a theater, bowling alley, basketball court,
and parking garage.

Compared to the tower, the church itself is remarkably plain,
ornamented only at the main portal tower and on the nearby chapel and
women's porches with sculptural programs executed by, among others,
the Piccirilli Brothers, sculptors of the Maine monument at Columbus
Circle. The interior is modelled on that of Chartres Cathedral, but
the nave is broader and less lofty than its French prototype. The stained
glass was mostly produced by Reynolds, Francis & Rohnstock of
Boston. Just off the main lobby is the chapel, a warmer, more intimate
and spiritual space.

Ⓑ General Grant National Memorial

122nd Street and Riverside Drive
1891–97 · JOHN H. DUNCAN

After some wrangling, New York won out over Washington, D.C., as
the final resting place for the eighteenth president and his wife.
A competition for a suitably monumental structure was held, and
Washington architect John Duncan's design was selected. The
Memorial was dedicated in 1897 by President McKinley, following a
parade the included 60,000 of the nation's soldiers and veterans.

A massive and somber cube rises from behind a Doric portico and
is crowned with a very substantial cylindrical drum and stepped dome.

The design draws heavily on French prototypes. This is particularly true inside, where Duncan channeled Napoleon's tomb at the Hôtel des Invalides in Paris. Like Napoleon, President and Mrs. Grant lie in red granite sarcophagi under the dome at the center of the cruciform space. Overhead, the pendentives are the work of sculptor J. Massey Rhind. They allegorically represent different moments in Grant's life. The three brightly colored figural mosaics in the tympana (1966) are by Allyn Cox.

The Memorial was restored and embellished under the auspices of the WPA in the 1930s. The floor and windows were replaced, and Federal Arts Project sculptors added busts of other Civil War generals to the crypt. It was at this point that the two eagles that flank the entrance moved here from their original home at New York's central post office opposite City Hall. The incongruous Rolling Bench around the tomb's perimeter is a New York City Public Art project executed in 1974 by Pedro Silva with the help of community volunteers.

Nearby, on the west side of Riverside Drive just north of 122nd Street, is the poignant and modest **Amiable Child Monument C**. "Erected to the Memory of an Amiable Child, St. Claire Pollock, Died 15 July 1797 in the Fifth Year of His Age." There could be no more affecting contrast than the one between the grandiose Grant Memorial and this forthright remembrance of a much-loved child.

West 154th

West 153rd

West 152nd

West 151st

West 150th

West 149th

West 148th

West 147th

West 146th

West 145th

West 144th

West 143rd

West 142nd

West 141st

West 140th

West 139th

West 138th

West 137th

West 136th

West 135th

West 134th

West 133rd

West 132nd

West 131st

West 130th

West 129th

West 128th

West 125th

Tiemann Place

La Salle

West 123rd

West 122nd

West 121st

Riverside Drive

Claremont Avenue

Amsterdam Avenue

Saint Nicholas Place

Hamilton Terrace

Convent Avenue

Hamilton Place

Old Broadway

1. 125th Street Viaduct
2. Old Broadway Synagogue
3. St. Mary's Episcopal Church
4. Prentis Hall
5. The Forum
6. Lenfest Center for the Arts and Jerome L. Greene Science Center
7. The Studebaker Building
8. Warren-Nash Automobile Parts Warehouse
9. Riverside Park Community
10. Claremont Theater

A. 135th Street Gatehouse
B. Bernard and Anne Spitzer School of Architecture
C. New York Training School for Teachers/New York Model School
D. City College
E. The Grange
F. St. Luke's Episcopal Church

11. Leslie Court
12. Cromwell Apartments
13. Ellerslie Court
14. Wingate Hotel
15. Rockclyffe Apartments
16. Garnet Hall
17. At Washington Court
18. Hamilton Theater
19. Ethelbert Court
20. Southold and Northold apartments
21. Halidon Court
22. Church of St. Catherine of Genoa

122nd Street to 153rd Street

Something dramatic happens when Broadway, sloping steeply down from Morningside Heights, arrives at 122nd Street: the subway tracks emerge from underground. The ground drops away below them, and the **125th Street Viaduct** ❶ carries the trains on a level course over the Manhattanville Valley.

The IRT designers turned a geographical necessity into an opportunity. At both its north and south ends, the 2,174-foot viaduct runs on a simple trestle, supported by walls in brick with boldly rusticated granite piers. At the midpoint, engineer William Barclay Parsons designed a parabolic steel arch that strides over 125th Street.

Take a look at the massive hinges that support the arches as they meet the ground. The steel beams, creosoted ties, and shining tracks silhouetted against the sky create complex patterns of light and dark, sun and shadow. The passenger bridges and escalators branch out from the station platform and descend to the street on either side of Broadway like the legs of a giant insect. Then look north and south at the perspectival recession of the tracks as they disappear into the hillside.

The subway viaduct crosses 125th Street obliquely. Because of the lay of the land, both the city's grid pattern and street numbering become complex in this area. A natural valley separates Morningside Heights to the south from Hamilton Heights to the north. This geological fault line extends east from the Hudson River at an angle. In early days, a street called The Hollow Way followed its path. Renamed

203

Manhattan Street, this route was the main thoroughfare for the thriving industrial hamlet of Manhattanville. When the grid was extended north, Manhattan Street did not line up. The solution, adopted in 1920, was to combine Manhattan Street with 125th Street into a single thoroughfare. Today 125th Street follows a diagonal course to Convent Avenue, where it angles to the left to align with the grid.

To further confuse matters other streets in the area, such as 126th, also take a diagonal course or disappear unexpectedly. There is even a street called Old Broadway that runs roughly parallel (with an interruption) to its contemporary namesake from 125th to 133rd Streets. This was the route followed by the Bloomingdale Road before it was straightened and regularized.

At 15 Old Broadway is the modest brick **Old Broadway Synagogue** ❷, built in 1923 to serve a growing population of Russian and Polish immigrants and an active center for Orthodox worship and education today. At the corner of Old Broadway and West 126th Street is **St. Mary's Episcopal Church** ❸ (1908, Theodore Blake with Carrère & Hastings) a parish church whose handsome brickwork, oversize west window, side entry porch, and small belfry breathes the spirit of the English Gothic Revival.

Between 123nd and 133rd Streets and set back from Broadway by a continuous brick wall and lawn are three public housing projects: Morningside Gardens, General U.S. Grant Houses, and the Manhattanville Houses, built in the late 1950s. The buildings determinedly turned their backs on Broadway. All sense of neighborhood and street life disappeared, and the complexes quickly became among the most dangerous and troubled in the city. Today the east side of the avenue is still bleak and forlorn, while beyond barrier of the viaduct, the west side is packed with lively restaurants and businesses with apartments above.

The corner of Broadway and 125th Street is the heart of Manhattanville, until recently a neighborhood composed primarily of factories and warehouses. **Prentis Hall** ❹ at 632 West 125th Street (1909, Frank Rooke) is a reminder of that history. Now a Columbia University classroom building, the once-gleaming white terra-cotta facade was a good match for the building's original tenant—a milk company.

❺ The Forum

601 West 125th Street
2018 · RENZO PIANO BUILDING
WORKSHOP WITH DATTNER
ARCHITECTS AND CAPLES
JEFFERSON ARCHITECTS

The wedge-shaped Forum was
designed as the gateway to
Columbia's new campus, a
setting for academic and public
conferences, meetings, and symposia. Inside are seminar rooms, social
spaces, and a 430-seat auditorium. The concrete prow of the Forum's
upper floors projects dramatically toward the intersection of Broadway
and 125th Street. Closer to street level a suspended canopy protects the
corner entry. The ground level is completely glazed, lifting and lightening
the solid mass above.

❻ Lenfest Center for the Arts and Jerome L. Greene Science Center

3227 Broadway
2016 · RENZO PIANO BUILDING
WORKSHOP WITH DAVIS BRODY
BOND AND BODY LAWSON
ASSOCIATES

The Lenfest Center is crisp,
white, and cubic, with upper floors
cantilevering boldly into space. It
is screened from Broadway by the
transparent Greene Science Center with its interior visible through
multilayered glass facades. Behind the smooth, taut facades is a
balanced network of ribs, beams,
and cables. The Science Center,
filled with light and air, seems to
float whether seen from the street

or from a passing train. Both buildings open onto a sheltered piazza, a
characteristic element of Piano's work.

To the north, work is currently underway on buildings for Columbia's new business school, designed by Diller Scofidio + Renfro in collaboration with FxCollaborative Architects and Harlem-based AARRIS ATEPA Architects. The Manhattanville campus will also include older adapted buildings. The **Studebaker Building** ❼ (1923), an auto finishing plant at 615 West 131st Street, still has its terra-cotta corporate logo in place on the western tower. On the other side of the elevated tracks, another Columbia property, the **Warren-Nash Automobile Parts Warehouse** ❽ at 3280 Broadway (1927) has a dignified masonry facade in cream and red.

Continuing up the hill, this part of Broadway seems curiously deserted. One reason may be the hulking presence of another inward-looking public housing project. The 1,200 apartments of the **Riverside Park Community** ❾ fill the west side of Broadway from 133rd to 135th Streets.

❿ Claremont Theater

3320 Broadway

1913–14 · GAETAN AJELLO

This theater was one of the first in the city specifically designed for motion pictures. The building originally also included a dance hall and roof garden. By 1933, the interior of the theater, which once seated 1,350 movie goers, had already been converted into an automobile showroom. Today

the Claremont soldiers on as a self-storage warehouse, albeit one with elegant classical detailing, including a relief of a motion picture camera in the garlanded cartouche over the main entry.

⬦ Convent Avenue/ City College

Two blocks east of Broadway is Convent Avenue, which is lined with the buildings of City College from 136th Street to 140th Street. On 135th Street are two buildings that have been repurposed for contemporary use.

Ⓐ 135th Street Gatehouse

150 Convent Avenue
1884–90 · FREDERICK S. COOK

By the late-nineteenth century, the city's need for fresh water had exceeded the capacity of the original Croton Aqueduct, and an expansion was undertaken. The 135th Street Gatehouse was a key distribution point for water entering the city from the new system. The gatehouse is remarkably powerful: massive, picturesque, and romantic in its studied asymmetry. Today the building has been converted into a theater for the Harlem Stage Company, while some of the exterior piping remains as a reminder of its original function.

Ⓑ Bernard and Anne Spitzer School of Architecture

141 Convent Avenue
1999–2009 · RAPHAEL VINOLY

Raphael Vinoly has converted a boxy 1930s-era campus library into a handsome home for City College's architecture school. Placed at a slight angle to the streets on a hilltop site, the

gleaming white and determinedly symmetrical building is crowned by a bright yellow rooftop amphitheater. It sits atop a five-story atrium at the center of the building.

◉ New York Training School for Teachers/ New York Model School

443 West 135th Street
1924–26 · WILLIAM H. GOMPERT

William Gompert succeeded C. B. J. Snyder as Superintendent of School Buildings. During his five-year term, Gompert oversaw the design and construction of some 170 academic buildings. This example accommodated three separate functions: a model school, a teacher training school, and a large gym and auditorium.

By 1897 **City College ◉** had outgrown its original home at Fourth Avenue and 23rd Street. Following the example of Columbia University, the college resolved to move uptown and acquired a dramatic site on St. Nicholas Terrace between 138th and 140th Streets overlooking

Harlem. Architect George B. Post won a competition to design the new campus in a Collegiate Gothic style that sought to evoke the glories of Oxford and Cambridge.

To keep costs down, Post built his complex from Manhattan schist quarried both on site and as part of the nearby excavations for the IRT subway. He set off the dark gray of the schist with white terra-cotta that was sand blasted to resemble stone. The vivid contrast between these materials allows the carefully studied detailing to make a striking impact.

Four academic buildings are arranged in a loose quadrangle facing the large Main Building, known today as **Shepard Hall**. With its dramatically projecting apse, twin towers, and curving wings, Shepard

Hall is a powerful statement about the ambitions of City College to make quality tuition-free education available to all.

Across the street, facing the quadrangle, the **Mechanic Arts Building** is easy to identify. It houses the college powerplant. Instead of hiding this fact, Post exploited it, boldly making the towering smokestack the focus of his composition. Throughout the quadrangle, terra-cotta reliefs and gargoyles enrich every building. Each carving alludes to the activities that went on inside. Post's embellishment reaches its peak on the campus gates with their remarkable and infinitely complex metal fretwork.

Walk around to the far side of Shepherd Hall for a look at its central tower and to take in the sweeping curve of the building along St. Nicholas Terrace. Alexander Hamilton's early nineteenth-century house, **The Grange ❺**, is nestled just down the hill on 141st Street. The house sat at the center of the thirty-two-acre estate that gives the Hamilton Heights neighborhood its name. The Grange has been moved twice, from its original site on 142nd Street to the churchyard of St. Luke's, and from there to its current location in 2008.

❻ St. Luke's Episcopal Church

281 Convent Avenue
1892 · R. H. ROBERTSON

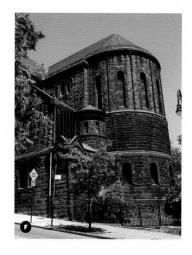

Here's a brownstone church of great solidity and ambitious scale, executed in a handsome Romanesque style. The compact massing of the volumes at the east end where the site slopes steeply down the hill is particularly satisfying. The church was initially intended to have a large tower over the portal at the corner of Convent Avenue, and a rich sculptural program was also planned. Today the building is shrouded in netting and awaiting restoration.

The blocks along Broadway from 135th to 153rd Street are lined with an almost unbroken series of six-story apartment houses. Nearly all of these were erected as speculative ventures during the extraordinary building boom that followed the completion of the IRT subway in 1904. These are not fancy buildings like the great apartment houses farther south, but more modest walk-up structures designed to appeal to middle-class workers who could now commute from their jobs in midtown to what was still a comparatively uncrowded and quiet neighborhood.

If the subway was the catalyst for the explosion of residential development along this section of Broadway, the basic design of the buildings themselves is principally due to the Tenement House Act of 1901. The Act included new legal requirements for improved apartment lighting, ventilation, sanitation, and fire safety.

The combination of new rules and the competitive pressure to get buildings up quickly resulted in apartment houses that were designed to a formula. In their eagerness to attract residents, however, developers worked to set their buildings apart. Each was assigned an evocative name, and architects were urged to vary their materials and to embellish their structures with fanciful terra-cotta ornament and cut-stone trim. The vast majority of the new buildings along this stretch of Broadway were designed by a small group of prolific apartment house specialists: Emery Roth, Schwartz & Gross, George F. Pelham, and, above all, Neville & Bagge.

Emery Roth's buildings such as **Leslie Court** ❶ at 3375 Broadway (1907) at 136th Street and the **Cromwell Apartments** ❷ at 3381 Broadway (1906) offer rich and inventive terra-cotta detailing, often influenced by the Vienna Secession. At the Cromwell, the fire escapes are recessed into the facade, spanning the resulting gap with segmental arches just below the cornice line. As with all too many buildings around the city, however, the original cornices of both buildings have been removed, leaving them looking impoverished and forlorn.

The entire block on the west side of Broadway between 138th and 139th Streets is the work of Neville & Bagge. All five buildings are in the firm's characteristic style: red brick, dramatically contrasting limestone

trim, strong projecting cornice. The same firm's handsome block-long **Ellerslie Court** ⓭ at 3441–59 Broadway between 140th and 141st Street employs the same materials and design vocabulary in a more subtle way.

On the east side of Broadway at 140th Street the **Wingate Hotel** ⓮ and neighboring **Rockclyffe Apartments** ⓯ (3440–3456 Broadway) by Schwartz & Gross achieve even more refined results with recessed fire escapes, deep light wells, and multicolored brick laid in Flemish bond.

Garnet Hall ⓰ at 3465–71 Broadway by Sommerfeld and Steckler shows another firm's approach to the same materials. Here the architects have forgone a dramatic cornice in favor of a striking fifth-floor corbel table and a richly decorated parapet.

On the east side of Broadway just south of 142nd Street is a group of five three-story row houses that date to 1892, before the arrival of the subway.

At **Washington Court** ⓱, 3504–18 Broadway, Neville & Bagge depart from their usual formula. Corner towers anchor either end of

a block-long building executed in light glazed brick. The distinctive detailing of the window surrounds on the upper floor takes its inspiration from the Spanish Renaissance. The other three corners at Broadway and 144th Street are occupied by nearly matching buildings by George F. Pelham, also executed in light brick.

In the early years of the twentieth century there was a movie theater every couple of blocks in this neighborhood. Today only one theater building remains.

⓲ Hamilton Theater

3560 Broadway
1913 · THOMAS W. LAMB

Now vacant, this building was designed by the celebrated theater architect Thomas Lamb at the height of the theater-building boom. The Hamilton began life as a main-line vaudeville house. It was a part of the Moss/ Brill and later the celebrated B. F. Keith circuits. Over the years, it slowly declined. It was a film house until 1958, then a sports/boxing arena, and then a discotheque. With its cornice removed and its marquee stripped away, the building today is a shadow of its former self, but there is still some playful ornament to be seen: the female herms flanking the windows on the second floor were clearly designed to attract business.

At 149th Street, the white-brick **Ethelbert Court ⑲**, 3621 Broadway, by Moore & Landsiedel offers Palladian arched balconies at the roof line. Their handsome original setting can still be seen on the side street where the flanking slanted roofs are still in place. In the next block, the **Southold** and **Northold** apartments ⑳ (1913), ten-story twins on the west side of Broadway, are more understated and disciplined than many of their neighbors. These upscale elevator buildings are significantly more luxurious than their six-story neighbors.

There are six more three-story row houses (1895) on the east side of Broadway just north of 151st Street. Emery Roth's **Halidon Court ㉑** (1910) is diagonally across the street at 3681 Broadway. The open corner site with unbroken views over Trinity Cemetery seems to have inspired Roth to let his imagination run free. There are art nouveau brackets, carved stone reliefs, brick mosaic panels, and exuberant bronze gutters. Somehow, they all work together to make an improbable but pleasing ensemble.

㉒ Church of St. Catherine of Genoa

504 West 153rd Street
1890 · THOMAS POOLE

Poole was an English-born architect who designed a number of Roman Catholic churches in New York, including the Church of the Holy Name on 96th Street and St. Thomas the Apostle, on 118th Street in Harlem. At St. Catherine, he has managed to squeeze into a single structure a touch of medieval Venice here, some Flemish gables there, and a bit of English Arts and Crafts on the porch.

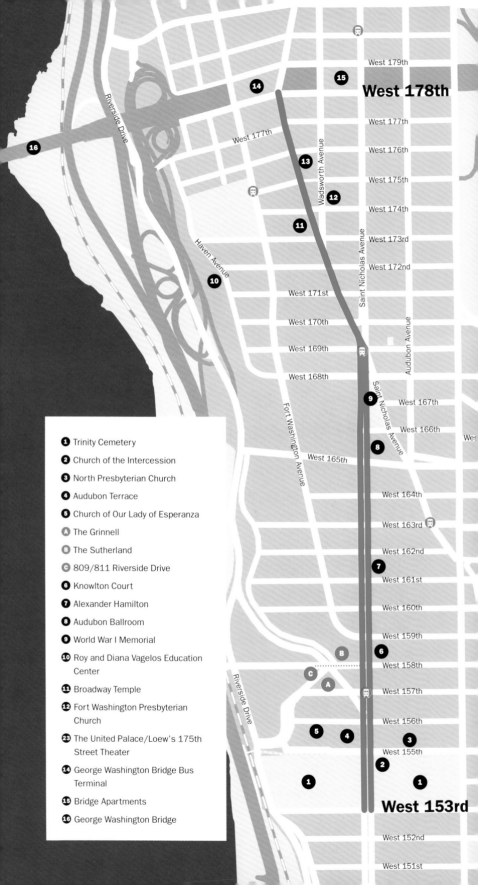

West 179th
West 178th
West 177th
West 176th
West 175th
West 174th
West 173rd
West 172nd
West 171st
West 170th
West 169th
West 168th
West 167th
West 166th
Wes
West 165th
West 164th
West 163rd
West 162nd
West 161st
West 160th
West 159th
West 158th
West 157th
West 156th
West 155th

West 153rd

West 152nd
West 151st

Riverside Drive
West 177th
Haven Avenue
Wadsworth Avenue
Saint Nicholas Avenue
Audubon Avenue
Fort Washington Avenue
Saint Nicholas Avenue
Riverside Drive

1 Trinity Cemetery

2 Church of the Intercession

3 North Presbyterian Church

4 Audubon Terrace

5 Church of Our Lady of Esperanza

A The Grinnell

B The Sutherland

C 809/811 Riverside Drive

6 Knowlton Court

7 Alexander Hamilton

8 Audubon Ballroom

9 World War I Memorial

10 Roy and Diana Vagelos Education Center

11 Broadway Temple

12 Fort Washington Presbyterian Church

23 The United Palace/Loew's 175th Street Theater

14 George Washington Bridge Bus Terminal

15 Bridge Apartments

16 George Washington Bridge

153rd Street to 178th Street

As Broadway climbs up the hill towards 153rd Street, it leaves behind the land of Alexander Hamilton and enters that of John James Audubon. For the next twenty-five blocks his name is everywhere. Trinity Cemetery is a perfect introduction to the neighborhood that was once the estate of this great naturalist.

❶ Trinity Cemetery

**East and west sides of
Broadway, between 153rd and
155th Streets**
1841 · JAMES RENWICK

In 1841, with its own churchyard on lower Broadway at capacity, Trinity Church needed additional burial space. The church bought a 23-acre tract of land overlooking the Hudson in the hamlet then known as Carmansville. The sloping site came not only with great views, but with a good dose of history: it was the scene of much of the action in the Battle of Washington Heights during the Revolutionary War. Trinity engaged James Renwick to lay out the cemetery in landscaped terraces, creating a park-like setting with specimen trees, walkways for strolling, and picturesque vistas. The first burials took place in 1843. Today, Trinity is the only active cemetery in Manhattan.

For thirty years, the cemetery remained an isolated country retreat, accessible from Midtown mainly by boat. In 1870, however, construction of the Boulevard reached 153rd Street and ran into Trinity's graveyard. The path of the road was not to be altered. Graves were relocated, rock blasted away, retaining walls erected, and the Boulevard proceeded north, straight through the center of the cemetery. In an effort to return some unity to its now divided property, Trinity commissioned Calvert Vaux to create a Gothic suspension bridge over the Boulevard. This remarkable structure remained in place until 1911, when it was removed to make way for the building of the Chapel (now Church) of the Intercession.

Trinity Cemetery remains an oasis. The entrance is at the bottom of the hill on West 155th Street. Once through the notable Gothic ironwork of the perimeter fence, there are fine views of the river and the George Washington Bridge. Among the notable New Yorkers buried here are Clement Clarke Moore (author of "The Night Before Christmas"), Eliza Jumel (wife of Aaron Burr), real estate magnate John Jacob Astor and his family, railway tycoon Jay Gould and his family, author Ralph Ellison, actor Jerry Orbach, and Mayor Ed Koch. John James Audubon himself is buried under a handsome Celtic cross.

❷ Church of the Intercession

550 West 155th Street

1910–14 · BERTRAM GROSVENOR GOODHUE OF CRAM, GOODHUE & FERGUSON

Dramatically sited, ambitiously conceived, and beautifully detailed, this imposing church is the work of Bertram Grosvenor Goodhue, who also designed, with his partner Ralph Adams Cram, St. Bartholomew's Church on Park Avenue and St. Thomas's on Fifth Avenue.

The Intercession congregation had been a fixture of the Carmansville neighborhood since 1846, occupying a series of buildings. In 1906, facing financial difficulties, Intercession affiliated itself with Trinity Church, which was looking to erect a chapel on the grounds of its cemetery. In addition to the church itself, the complex includes an intimate vaulted cloister, a parish house, and a charming vicarage.

The Church of the Intercession was the architect's favorite building. (He is buried in the crypt.) With its soaring facade facing Broadway, an asymmetrical tower anchoring the complex on the north, and its evocative cluster of subsidiary buildings, it

manages to be both robust and elegant. Take a moment to admire the quality of the carving and stonework on the portals. There is a beautiful balance between the soft gray ashlar walls and the bright limestone trim. Inside, the nave is impressive in its scale and dignity. If it is open, the crypt is also worth a visit.

In 1976 Intercession dissolved its affiliation with Trinity. Today the active, independent congregation is focused on serving its neighborhood.

❸ North Presbyterian Church

525 West 155th Street
1904 · BANNISTER & SCHELL

Three congregations merged and moved here just after the turn of the century to build this impressive new home: a 1,000-seat sanctuary and an ample parish house separated from each other by an ambitious Gothic tower. The church makes a fine impression from the street, but look carefully at the peaked roof over the large window. It extends back only a short distance. The actual roof of the balconied preaching hall is flat.

❹ Audubon Terrace

West side of Broadway, 155th to 156th Streets
1904–30 · CHARLES PRATT HUNTINGTON AND OTHERS

Archer Huntington, stepson of transcontinental railway builder Collis P. Huntington, was an enthusiastic patron of the arts and a serious scholar. He was also a visionary. Sensing a real estate opportunity and eager to erect a home for several learned societies of which he was a sponsor, Huntington conceived a plan to create an uptown acropolis—an architecturally unified campus of museums, libraries, and scholarly institutions. To this end, he acquired nearly a full square block of land from the family of John James Audubon.

Passionately devoted to the art and culture of Spain, Archer Huntington began by founding the **Hispanic Society of America**. He engaged his cousin Charles P. Huntington to design a home for the society and to draw up a master plan for the entire site based on Beaux-Arts principles. Buildings for the **American Numismatic Society** (1907), the **American Geographic Society** (1911), the **Museum of the American Indian, Heye Foundation** (1915–22), the **American Academy of Arts and Letters** (1921–23, McKim, Mead & White), and the **National Institute of Arts and Letters** (1928–30, Cass Gilbert) were all duly erected. Huntington's plan also included a small church: **Our Lady of Esperanza** (1909, Charles P. Huntington; remodeled 1925).

Huntington's original site plan oriented the buildings to face 156th Street with a central approach up a wide and stately flight of steps. With the architect's death in 1919, however, the plan changed. The main entrance was relocated to Broadway. As a result, the buildings, all arranged around a central plaza, were approached from the side rather than head-on as initially envisioned. Today, with the exception of the Hispanic Society and the Academy of Arts and Letters, all the original tenants have relocated. Some buildings are closed, others have been repurposed.

The Hispanic Society is filled with masterpieces by Velasquez, Ribera, and Murillo. Joaquin Sorolla's cycle of murals depicting the regions of Spain is unforgettable in its dazzling brushwork and brilliant color. On the plaza outside are sculptures by Archer Huntington's wife, Anna Hyatt Huntington.

It's also worth visiting the **Church of Our Lady of Esperanza ❺** (624 West 156th Street). The church was only the second in New York built specifically to serve a Spanish-speaking congregation. It continues to do so today.

⬦ Audubon Park

The **Audubon Park Historic District** lies to the west of Broadway between 155th and 158th Streets. This enclave sits almost entirely on "Minnie's Land"— the 20-acre estate of John James Audubon and his wife, Minnie. After Audubon's death in 1851 his estate began to sell off parcels of land, a practice that continued into the twentieth century.

Development proceeded slowly until the arrival of the subway. At this point, the combination of an attractive site overlooking the river and the proximity of such distinguished neighbors as Trinity Cemetery and Audubon Terrace inspired developers to create an elegant new neighborhood. Unlike the section of Broadway to the south of the cemetery, this was to be a markedly upscale area. Work progressed quickly. Of the nineteen major apartment buildings in this historic district, nine were constructed between 1905 and 1910. The remainder were finished by 1932.

These buildings feature stylish entryways, ornately appointed lobbies, and spirited decorative detailing. Intended for prosperous occupants, the original apartments were very spacious, recalling those in the trend-setting buildings farther south on the Upper West Side.

The Grinnell ⓐ (800 Riverside Drive, 1910, Schwartz & Gross) seems to sail up the hill like the prow of a great ocean liner. Across the street, **The Sutherland ⓑ** (611 West 158th Street, 1909,

219

Emery Roth) evokes *fin de siècle* Paris, while the soaring, cliff-like light courts at the **Riviera** (790 Riverside Drive, 1909, Rouse and Goldstone) are dizzying. At **809–811 Riverside Drive ●** is a double house built in 1920 in a Mediterranean style by developer Nathan Berler. The red-brick villa with its green tile roof presents an alternative model for the development of the neighborhood, offering both the pleasures of city life and those of a freestanding house in the suburbs then emerging outside of Manhattan.

Each apartment house in the neighborhood has a distinctive and evocative name. These were intended to set a tone and to conjure up fashionable associations in the minds of prospective tenants. Some names nod to the history of the area (Audubon Hall, The Grinnell). Some speak to the allure of Europe (The Vauxhall, The Cragmoor, The Riviera, Crillon Court, The Sutherland). Others evoke areas of natural beauty (The Rhinecliff, The Kannawah), and still others gesture towards the presence of Huntington's new Hispanic Society nearby (Hispania Hall, The Cortez, The Goya, The Velasquez). The origin of the name Hortense Arms on the other hand, remains a mystery.

Moving north on Broadway, the streetscape is similar to the blocks south of Trinity Cemetery. Neville and Bagge's **Knowlton Court** ❻ at 3800–3810 Broadway turns mandatory fire escapes into decorative accents, while their **Alexander Hamilton** ❼ at 3860 Broadway features attractive terra-cotta window surrounds.

❽ Audubon Ballroom

3940 Broadway
1912 · THOMAS W. LAMB

At first glance it's hard to know what to make of the elaborate polychromed terra-cotta facade along the east side of Broadway at 165th Street. Above the central portal, King Neptune perches atop an imperial Roman galley bristling with oars and guided by a seductive mermaid. This impressive sculptural group sails boldly out over the sidewalk. The rest of the facade features elegant mosaic panels and fanciful ornament, including pilasters adorned with images of a fox. A modern office tower, erected in 1992 for Columbia University, rises incongruously behind this festive arched ensemble.

The preserved facade once belonged to a large theater and ballroom combination designed in 1912 by Thomas Lamb for William Fox of 20th-Century Fox—hence the foxes. Over the years the building (under a variety of names) was home to vaudeville and movies. By the 1940s the ballroom was a popular setting for political and union rallies. Tragically, it was here on February 21, 1965, that human rights activist Malcolm X was assassinated as he began to address his followers. In subsequent years the Audubon fell on hard times. After a protracted battle preservationists and developers reached a compromise. The existing section of the facade was preserved along with a portion of the ballroom. In 2005 the building reopened as the Malcolm X and Dr. Betty Shabazz Memorial and Education Center.

Just north of the Audubon Ballroom at 166th Street is a triangle of land between Broadway and St. Nicholas Avenue. This is **Mitchel Square**, named in honor of John Purroy Mitchel, the youngest person to serve as New York's mayor, elected in 1913 at age 34. He died training for service in World War I. In this context, it seems appropri-

ate that Mitchel Square is the site of the **Washington Heights-Inwood World War I Memorial ❾** (1922), designed by sculptor, art patron, and museum founder Gertrude Vanderbilt Whitney. Whitney worked in France with the Red Cross during the war. Upon her return to the United States, she exhibited a series of small sculptures entitled *Impressions of War* inspired by her experiences abroad. The design for the Washington Heights Memorial was included as a part of that series. In the executed work, Whitney neatly addresses the challenges of an exposed site by creating a spiraling, stepped composition of three figures that reads equally well from all sides. Instead of adhering to the prevailing preference for memorials that stressed triumph or valor, Whitney shows actual suffering. The neighborhood had lost 347 men in the conflict.

The vast hilltop campus of **Columbia Presbyterian Medical Center** dominates this section of Manhattan. The American flag at the top of the main building is a highly visible landmark from all directions. The Columbia University Medical School and Presbyterian Hospital moved their joint facility here in the mid-1920s and commissioned James Gamble Rogers to design the new complex. Today Rogers' buildings seem solidly traditional, but at the time of their construction many critics regarded them as paragons of modernity.

The hospital has expanded continually over the past century. The most architecturally interesting building in the complex is the **Roy and Diana Vagelos Education Center** ⑩ (104 Haven Avenue, 2016, Diller Scofidio + Renfro in association with Gensler). Study spaces cascade down the south facade in an unbroken flow. More traditional classrooms and labs, as well as the elevator core, are to the north. Off to the west there is an appealing terrace overlooking the Hudson.

On another note, beginning in 1903 the current hospital site was the location of Hilltop Park, home to New York's American League baseball team, the Highlanders. With their departure from Washington Heights in 1912 the team got a new name: the New York Yankees.

At 169th Street, Broadway intersects with St. Nicholas Avenue, the route of the Old Bloomingdale and Kingsbridge Roads. Here Broadway veers off to the west, following the path of the Kingsbridge Road to the Harlem River at 221st Street. More than anything else, the route is determined by geography, moving through the valley between the highlands along the Hudson to the west and the bluffs of Fort George to the east. The IRT subway, which has run below Broadway from Times Square, now continues straight under St. Nicholas Avenue until 218th Street.

169th Street also marks the spot where the Boulevard came to an end. For the past 100 blocks Broadway has been a wide thoroughfare with an ample planted median and broad sidewalks. At 169th Street the median disappears, and Broadway begins to look more like other avenues.

⑪ Broadway Temple–United Methodist Church of Washington Heights

4111 Broadway

1927 · DONN BARBER

1947–52 · SHREVE, LAMB & HARMON

This modest complex was intended to be far grander. In the mid-1920s the Methodist Church of Washington Heights learned that its building at Fort Washington Avenue and 178th Street was scheduled for demolition to make way for the new George Washington Bridge. The Rev. Christian Reisner saw this as an opportunity to blend religion and revenue in a modern way. He commissioned architect Donn Barber to design a 40-story skyscraper church on Broadway between 173rd and 174th Streets. This "temple" was to include apartments, a hotel, a recreation center with a pool and bowling alleys, and a new church sanctuary seating 2,000 worshippers. The complex was to be topped with a rotating 75-foot cross.

Work was completed on the two existing apartment buildings, designed to flank the soaring main tower. The Depression, however, soon brought the project to a halt. By 1947 outstanding debts had been settled and work resumed on a much-reduced project. The proposed skyscraper tower was replaced by the current church designed by Shreve, Lamb & Harmon.

Visible above the storefronts on the east side of Broadway is the dramatic, over-scaled tower of the **Fort Washington Presbyterian Church** ⑫ (21 Wadsworth Ave, 1914, Thomas Hastings of Carrère and Hastings). This English-inspired design with its handsome portico recalls the eighteenth-century work of Nicholas Hawksmoor.

⑬ The United Palace/ Loew's 175th Street Theater

4140 Broadway

1930 · THOMAS W. LAMB; INTERIORS BY HAROLD RAMBUSCH

The east side of Broadway at 174th Street is dominated by what was once one of New York's great movie palaces.

Loew's 175th Street opened in 1930 as the last of five Wonder Theaters built as flagship venues for the famous chain. It was designed to dazzle. Like its companions (Kings Theater in Brooklyn, the Paradise in the Bronx, the Valencia in Queens, and the Jersey in Jersey City), its interior is an exuberant blend of architectural styles described by architectural writer David Dunlap as "Byzantine-Romanesque-Indo-Hindu-Sino-Moorish-Persian-Eclectic-Rococo-Deco." The 3,400-seat auditorium, complete with its Wonder Morgan

organ, was designed by theater architect Thomas Lamb. The interior decoration is the work of Harold Rambusch, who lent his talents to the Roxy and Hollywood Theaters. He was also the designer of the more refined interiors of the Waldorf-Astoria Hotel and Radio City Music Hall.

The theater opened with a Norma Shearer film and stage show; it closed in March 1969 with *2001: A Space Odyssey*. Almost immediately the building was purchased by radio-evangelist Frederick J. Eikerenkoetter, "Reverend Ike," as a base for his Prosperity Ministry.

Today the theater is the home of The United Palace House of Inspiration (UPHI), which also operates a community cultural center in the building. In recent decades, stage shows have returned to the United Palace. And thanks to a focused community effort led by composer/performer Lin-Manuel Miranda, periodic film screenings have also come back to the theater.

Three blocks ahead, a sunken expressway slices across
Manhattan from the George Washington Bridge to the Bronx.
In addition to the remarkable network of interlocking ramps,
viaducts, and cloverleafs that link it to other highways,
two major architectural projects were designed as integral
components of the expressway project: the George Washington
Bridge Bus Terminal and the Bridge Apartments.

⑭ George Washington Bridge Bus Terminal

4211 Broadway

1963 · PIER LUIGI NERVI

This is a mid-twentieth-century
counterpart to Santiago
Calatrava's contemporary
Oculus downtown at the World
Trade Center—a distinctively
designed building by an
international architect that
combines a shopping center with
a transportation hub. Nervi's
two-story terminal straddles the expressway and is a powerful, almost
overwhelming presence in the neighborhood. The Italian architect's
truss designs are innovative, and his use of concrete is bold and
sculptural. Notice in particular the dramatic wedge-shaped air vents
that angle upward and outward from the center of the roof.

At 178th Street Broadway passes between the two wings of the
terminal. Overhead are a pair of angled bridges, separated by
an opening to the sky. The southern bridge is straight, but Nervi has
curved the northern bridge giving the opening a dynamic irregular
shape. At street level, a winged canopy on the west side signals the
location of the entry. The previously dingy interior was handsomely
renovated in 2017. There are new waiting areas, and unused sections
of the building have been adapted for retail use.

To the east of the bus terminal are the four 32-story towers of the **Bridge Apartments** ⑮, designed in 1963 by the firm of Brown & Guenther. Somehow the developers convinced themselves that it made sense to place apartments over twelve lanes of motor traffic, bathed twenty-four hours a day in exhaust fumes and pummeled with noise. Not surprisingly, the apartments are barely habitable.

It's worth concluding this walk with a short detour to the west to look at the **George Washington Bridge** ⑯. Othmar Ammann's powerful design (1927–31) is an engineering and aesthetic triumph. Every year over 100 million vehicles cross, making the GWB the world's busiest vehicular bridge. It is a key crossing point not only for Manhattan-bound traffic, but also for cars, trucks, and buses headed to the Bronx and then on to New England.

Harlem River

West 220th
West 219th
West 218th
West 216th
West 215th
West 213th
West 212th
West 211th
West 207th
West 204th

Indian Road
Seaman Avenue
Park Terrace West
Park Terrace East
9th Ave
Payson Avenue
Academy
Cumming
Dyckman
Cooper
Vermilyea Avenue
Sherman Avenue
Post Avenue
Nagle Avenue
10th Avenue

University Heights Bridge

Thayer
Arden
Sickles
Ellwood
West 196th
Nagle Avenue
Bogardus Place
Hillside
Dongan Place

Broadway Terrace
Fairview Avenue
Wadsworth Terrace
Bennett Avenue

West 192nd
West 191st
West 190th
West 189th
West 188th
West 187th
West 187th
West 186th
West 186th
West 185th
West 184th
West 184th
West 183rd
West 182nd
West 181st
West 180th
West 179th

Wadsworth Avenue
Saint Nicholas Ave.
Audubon Avenue
Amsterdam Avenue

Washington Bridge

West 178th

West 177th

1. 4249 Broadway
2. Coliseum Theater
3. 34th Precinct station house
4. Police Officer Michael J. Buczek School
5. 4410 and 4420 Broadway
6. 191st Street Station
7. 4580 Broadway
8. Intermediate School 218/Salome Urena de Henriquez School
9. Packard garage
10. Tryon Gardens
11. 4720 Broadway
12. Broaddyke Apartments
13. Hawthorne Gardens
14. The Stack
15. Dyckman Farmhouse
16. Church of the Good Shepherd
17. Park Terrace Gardens
18. Campbell Sports Center
19. New York Presbyterian's Allen Hospital
20. Broadway Bridge

178th Street to the Harlem River

By the time Broadway reaches 178th Street, the transformation that began at 169th Street is complete. North of the George Washington Bridge, traffic is concentrated in the slender valley between the western heights of Fort Tryon Park and those of Fort George to the east. Just past the bus terminal, Broadway begins a gradual descent towards Inwood. Residential development is less dense, with large apartment buildings clustered along Fort Washington Avenue to the west or along St. Nicholas Avenue to the east. After about ten blocks of filling stations, garages, and tire shops interspersed with other businesses and civic buildings, residential development returns. This is the result of the arrival in 1932 of the IND subway line and a subsequent building boom along the final stretch of Broadway.

Walking north, the Citibank branch at **4249 Broadway** ❶ is one of a number of similar limestone buildings that Walker & Gilette designed for the National City Bank in the late 1920s. Next door, on the southwest corner of Broadway

and 181st Street, is a larger streamlined classical bank. The building with its angled corner has been colonized by a variety of retail tenants.

❷ Coliseum Theater

701 West 181st Street

1920 · EUGENE DE ROSA

This 3,500-seat movie and vaudeville house (one of the largest in the city at its opening) operated with success for decades, featuring the likes of Harold Lloyd, Ethel Waters, Eddie Cantor, Milton Berle, Bob Hope, and even Rin-Tin-Tin. In a now-familiar pattern of declining fortunes and multiple adaptations, it finally closed in 2011. Today so many changes and accretions have taken place

that it is easy to walk by the site without identifying it as a former movie palace. The delicate fan-shaped reliefs on the 181st Street side are a reminder of days gone by.

An interesting historical note: this is the location of the once-famous Blue Bell Tavern, a major site in the history of the Revolutionary War during the struggle for control of Manhattan Island. Remains of the tavern were still visible on this corner until construction of the theater in 1920.

At 183rd Street the west side of Broadway is dominated by the powerful, blocky red-brick presence of the **34th Precinct station house ❸**. Three blocks further along the **Police Officer Michael J. Buczek School ❹** (1992), is named in honor of one of New York's Finest, who was killed in the line of duty in 1988. This is a cheerful and welcoming design, warmly detailed in cream and orange brick. The letters of the alphabet on the facade are a charming touch.

At **4410** and **4420 Broadway** ❺ (1938, H. Herbert Lillien) represent a new configuration for apartment houses, one that will reappear in the blocks ahead. Instead of completely covering the buildable lot, these buildings sit back from the street with open entry courtyards, a luxury made possible by the lower cost of land in upper Manhattan.

The entrance to the **191st Street Station ❻** of the #1 train is on the east side of the street just north of Amelia Gorman Park. The

brightly painted portal provides access to a two-block-long tunnel, every inch covered with murals by four local artists, sponsored by the MTA Art & Design program. At the end of the tunnel is the deepest subway station in the city.

About three blocks ahead, where Bennett Avenue enters on the west, Broadway nestles up against the eastern edge of Fort Tryon Park. In the next block, past another freestanding red brick open-courtyard apartment at 4580 Broadway ❼ (1937, H.I. Feldman), is **Intermediate School 218/Salome Urena de Henriquez School** ❽ (1989, Richard Dattner), named for the nineteenth-century Dominican poet and educator. Its curving wings spread confidently outward, framing a glazed central stair tower.

Half a block further along, where Sherman Avenue branches off to the east, is a surprisingly elegant **parking garage** ❾ on the corner. Its gracefully curved facade and fine classic detailing seem incongruous until you pick out the faded word "Packard" on the cornice. The building was designed in 1926 by Albert Kahn, whose name is so closely tied to innovative factories and showrooms for the automobile industry. When it was erected, the garage was the luxury brand's central New York sales and service facility.

The next several blocks around Dongan Place and Arden Street feature some unusually handsome art deco apartment houses, all erected in the mid-1930s following the opening of the IND subway line. The buildings of **Tryon Gardens** ⑩ at 4690 and 4700 Broadway are particularly handsome, facing each other across a landscaped courtyard. On the next corner, Arden Street, **4720 Broadway** ⑪ (1935, Horace Ginsbern) features wrap-around Bauhaus-inspired windows, cheerful colored brickwork, and brick pilasters that rise the full height of the building to stylish abstracted capitals.

At Dyckman Street, Broadway angles to the east and begins an uninterrupted run to the Harlem River through the Inwood neighborhood. Like 125th Street to the south, Dyckman Street passes east–west between the Hudson and Harlem Rivers in a natural valley that separates the hills of Fort Tryon Park from those of Inwood Hill Park at the northern tip of Manhattan Island. Isolated by its natural geography, the Inwood neighborhood seems a community apart. The vast majority of buildings here were built in the 1920s and 30s. Very little rebuilding has taken place, so the neighborhood is remarkably uniform in style.

As it moves north from Dyckman Street, Broadway divides Inwood into two distinct parts. To the west the land rises to rocky cliffs overlooking the river. These heights were long the home of private country estates for the Billings, Seaman, and Isham families. Today the land is shared by attractive apartment buildings and parks. To the east of Broadway, the land is flat and low-lying. This was once rich farmland; today it is chiefly given over to more modest tenements and to one of the city's largest subway yards.

Just beyond Dyckman Street, look into the courtyard of the handsome **Broadyke Apartments** ⑫ (1927, Franklin, Bates, & Heindsman) at 4761 Broadway. A few steps from the bustle of the street, the peaceful courtyard provides access to the

building's several entrances. **Hawthorne Gardens** ⓭, further along at Broadway and Academy Street, has a similar plan. Across Broadway, between Dyckman and Cumming Streets, look for the colorful barnyard animals along the roofline of the Fine Fare Market.

⓮ The Stack

4857 Broadway
2013 · GLUCK+

This sleek seven-story is among New York's first modular apartment houses. Twenty-eight rental apartments, were each fabricated off site and then assembled here in less than four weeks. It's a good solution for this mid-block site, respecting the scale and roofline of its neighbors.

⓯ Dyckman Farmhouse

4881 Broadway

This is the only eighteenth-century farmhouse left in Manhattan. Around 1784 William Dyckman built his house at the center of a 250-acre farm, a replacement for an earlier home destroyed by the British during the Revolution. The fieldstone and clapboard house with its gambrel roof and strong Dutch character remained in the family until 1868 when it was sold. Nearly a half century later in 1915, two Dyckman descendants repurchased the property and undertook a restoration. The following year, they presented the house to the city, and it is now administered by the Historic House Trust, a public-private partnership.

The interior is open to the public. It contains an appealing and informative set of exhibitions about the neighborhood and its history. In the rear garden is a reconstructed Hessian Hut. During the Battle of Washington Heights in November 1776, a large contingent of German mercenary soldiers were housed on the Dyckman Farm in huts like this one.

As you leave the farmhouse, take note of the nicely preserved Covington Style lamp post, a variant on a special design created to light the Boulevard in the late nineteenth century. Along with the more familiar "Bishop's Crook" posts and a few more elaborate styles, nearly 100 of these evocative fixtures have been recognized as city landmarks. There are several functioning examples along this section of Broadway.

16 Church of the Good Shepherd

4967 Broadway

1935 · PAUL MONAGHAN

During the 1930s, due in large part to the arrival of the IND subway, Inwood's population grew rapidly, attracting a large number of Irish immigrants. This imposing Roman Catholic church with its attached school and convent was built to serve that community. Solidly constructed of stone in a modernized Romanesque style with well-carved portals and a tile roof, the large sanctuary can accommodate nearly 1,000 worshippers. Inside, the broad nave is spanned by a single stone barrel vault. This church breathes solidity and prosperity. It feels like what it long has been, the center of life in the neighborhood.

On the Isham Street side of the church is a memorial to the first responders who lost their lives at the World Trade Center in the wake of the terrorist attacks on September 11, 2001.

North of Isham Street, **Isham Park** fills the west side of Broadway. The sidewalk is bordered by a rubble stone wall, and mature trees overhang the walkway, creating a cool and shaded path. The Isham family donated the land to the city in 1912.

At 215th Street a steep flight of steps leads up the hill to the former site of the Seaman/Drake estate. Although the steps have been in place since 1911, their present handsome design dates to 2016 and incorporates two of the original lamp posts.

Around 1855 John Seaman, son of the man who introduced the smallpox vaccine to America, acquired this hilltop site. He built a massive white marble mansion with sweeping views over both the Hudson and Harlem Rivers. The house survived until 1938 when it was replaced by **Park Terrace**

Gardens, a carefully planned complex of five buildings with 400 units grouped around a lovely central garden. The architect was Albert Goldhammer. Today the sole remnant of the Seaman estate is the massive **triumphal arch** ⏺ that was once its entrance. If you look behind the weathered auto body repair shop on the west side of Broadway at 216th Street, you can see it standing in all its stalwart ruination.

⏺ Campbell Sports Center

Northwest corner of Broadway and 218th Street

2013 · STEVEN HOLL AND CHRIS MCVOY

From 218th Street north to the Harlem River, the west side of Broadway is dominated by Columbia University's Baker Sports Complex with the Campbell Sports Center as the gateway to the complex.

Holl used frankly industrial materials—sanded aluminum and glass—to create an arresting abstract composition of solids and voids, crisscrossed and broken up by the diagonals of the exterior stairways. In a nod to its architectural context, the stairs recall those of the nearby

20

subway stations and the materials of the adjacent viaducts. Hidden
behind the building are facilities for baseball, football, tennis, crew, and
soccer. Just past the soccer stadium bleachers, a curving drive leads
up to New York Presbyterian's **Allen Hospital** ⓳, the last building in
Manhattan.

Just ahead, both the road and the rails pass over the double-deck
Broadway Bridge ⓴, completed in 1962 close to the former site
of the Kings Bridge, the eighteenth-century crossing of the Harlem
River. The Harlem River is to the right, and Spuyten Duyvil Creek to
the left. In 1895 the original shallow, meandering creek was dredged
and straightened so that ships could move safely westward from the
Harlem River to the Hudson.

We have reached the upper tip of Manhattan island, the end of our
walk. But on the far side of the bridge, Broadway continues north.
As US Route 9, it passes through the Bronx, up the Hudson Valley, and
on through New York State to Canada.

Options for the End of the Walk

Walk across the bridge to the 225th Street IRT station. It provides an easy connection back downtown. The station is in Marble Hill, a neighborhood that was geographically attached to Manhattan before Spuyten Duyvil Creek was dredged. Although now physically in the Bronx, the neighborhood officially remains a part of Manhattan.

Explore **Inwood Hill Park.** Backtrack to 218th Street. From there, walk westward for about four blocks into the lower sections of the park. Here you can find a bench next to Spuyten Duyvil Creek, where there is a view of the Muscotta Marsh and the arched Henry Hudson Bridge.

Find the **Shorakkopoch Rock** and consider one of the enduring controversies of New York history: just where did the celebrated transaction in 1626 between Peter Minuit and the Indians take place? The plaque on the Inwood boulder stakes a claim that the deal was made here. On the other hand, there is a monument in Battery Park, just next to the Custom House, that suggests that the transaction took place at the start of our walk.

Visit **Fort Tryon Park.** It is easily accessed through the **Anne Loftus Playground** at the corner of Riverside Drive and Broadway (near the Dyckman Street stop of the A train). The park is home to **The Cloisters**, **Linden Terrace,** and the **Heather Garden**, all the gift to the city of John D. Rockefeller Jr.

Acknowledgments

Books like this don't just happen. I've relied heavily on the work of other authors, and I've been lucky enough to have had the enthusiastic support of and to have benefitted from the professional advice of friends, family, and a range of history and architecture specialists.

Thomas Mellins and Andrew Dolkart read the manuscript and offered invaluable insights and corrections for which I will be eternally grateful. Friends, New York enthusiasts, and fellow walkers Alfie Graham, Megan Rutherford, Carol Wallace, and Rick Hamlin have cheered me on and offered advice (as well as proofreading.) Ray Forsythe, Lisa Queen, and Judy Twersky provided support and informed perspective at crucial stages of the project. Carole Anne Fabian and Staff of Avery Library, Mary Beth Betts at NYC Design Commission, Donald Albrecht at the Museum of the City of New York, and Valerie Komor of the Associated Press were generous with their time and expertise. At The Monacelli Press Elizabeth White and her colleagues transformed the manuscript into a handsome work of art.

And then there is my family: my daughter, Claire Hennessey, my son-in-law, Andrew Thompson, and my extraordinary wife, Leslie Griffin Hennessey. Without their support, and insight, and sustained editorial effort this book would simply never have happened.

First published in the United States by The
Monacelli Press. All rights reserved.

Library of Congress Control Number
202093086
ISBN 978-158093-535-7

Design: Shawn Hazen, hazencreative.com

Printed in China

The Monacelli Press
6 West 18th Street
New York, New York 10011

Photography Credits

All photographs are by the author, except
as noted below:

Whitney Cox 172
Ilan Jacobsohn, 1999. Courtesy of the Art
Students League 144 bottom
Kenneth Grant/Newyorkitecture.com 151
Irving Underhill Collection, Museum of the
City of New York 8
Jonathan Wallen 72, 103 top left
Elizabeth White 110, 121 bottom